THE HIGH PRIESTLY PRAYER

THE
HIGH PRIESTLY PRAYER

A DEVOTIONAL COMMENTARY ON THE
SEVENTEENTH CHAPTER OF ST JOHN

By

H. C. G. MOULE, D.D.

A LIVING WORD MINISTRIES PUBLICATION

BAKER BOOK HOUSE
Grand Rapids, Michigan

Reprinted 1978 by
Baker Book House
from the edition issued in 1907 by
The Religious Tract Society

ISBN: 0-8010-6048-6

PHOTOLITHOPRINTED BY CUSHING - MALLOY, INC.
ANN ARBOR, MICHIGAN, UNITED STATES OF AMERICA
1978

Prefatory Note

MANY years ago, in my rooms in Trinity College, Cambridge, I read devotional papers on Sunday nights to gatherings of University men. One series of these readings was devoted to the great High Priestly Prayer.

More than a generation has passed, and I have re-read those papers and reviewed their line of exposition. Taking my old notes here and there for re-writing, and then again working in new directions, I have once more attempted a simple 'explanation' of the wonderful Chapter.

The work has awakened a thousand dear memories, and has also brought to my heart and mind a deep consciousness of the changes which, even since 1875, have passed over current religious thought and particularly over thought upon the Written Word. But I thank Him who is the same yesterday and to-day that a conscious-

The High Priestly Prayer

ness that 'the things which cannot be shaken do remain' is strong upon me after my second study. Among those things are the glory of the Only Begotten, the eternal certainty of His redemptive work, His living and prevailing advocacy, His present faithfulness and coming glory. Among them also is the firm conviction that 'He who spared not His Son' has not forgotten to give us, 'with Him,' the vital boon of an authentic record of what He was, and did, and said; that not in vain has His Church rested from earliest days on the sacred verity and veracity of the Fourfold Record; and that in the Words of Jesus so presented to us we have, for the repose of faith and the strength of hope, the precious possession of reports authorized by the Speaker.

HANDLEY DUNELM

AUCKLAND CASTLE
September 1907

Contents

The High Priestly Prayer

I

Preliminaries

IT is no light matter to attempt to deal as an expositor with the Seventeenth Chapter of St John. It is a Scripture which has well been called the Holy Place of the Bible; let him who would presume to comment upon it prepare himself by first, as it were, kneeling to worship at the threshold. The chapter bears commonly in Germany the title of 'the High Priestly Prayer,' as being the one prolonged utterance of our Lord recorded in the Scriptures in which He appears throughout as the Advocate, the Intercessor, engaged here on earth in the work which He now lives to do for us upon the Throne itself. Well may the would-be commentator betake himself first to the Intercessor for mercy, grace, and light.

The High Priestly Prayer

In the Readings now to follow I am not about to attempt any critical work, in the commonly understood sense of critical. I shall take the Greek words as they stand in the Testament, and render them simply into English, and treat them with reverence and faith as the very utterance and phrase of our Lord Jesus Christ, spoken 'in the same night in which He was betrayed.' I do this not because I forget the questions raised by literary criticism, to an unexampled degree in our day, over well-nigh every page of every Gospel. Least of all can I forget that around the last Gospel, with its altogether peculiar characteristics, the literary conflict has been waged, for two or three generations now, with a singular keenness and persistency, and the attempt to regard it as a sacred and sublime romance rather than a record has come to the front again lately in a new degree. But I think that the believer in our Lord Jesus Christ may still study the Fourth Gospel in peace as the authentic report of his Lord's acts and words,

Preliminaries

preserved for us by His chosen friend. I say this partly as one who thinks that no 'new light' has *really* put out of date the work of such students as Lightfoot, Westcott, and Ezra Abbot in literary vindication of the trustworthiness of that Gospel.[1] But partly, and mainly, I go down further for the basis of my confidence. I am persuaded for myself—imposing no conclusions of mine on others, but only stating them—that 'He that spared not His Son, but gave Him up for us all,' may be trusted, on grounds large and deep, to have 'given us with Him also' the boon of solidity and veracity in the only records which have come down to us, from a primeval date, with the presumption of authenticity. I take the four Gospels, all the four, and I examine them, at first, as far as I can by sincere mental efforts, *without* the presupposition of their supernatural verity, and lay myself out simply to receive

Rom. viii. 32

---

[1] See also the much more recent and singularly independent work, Dr James Drummond's *Character and Authorship of the Fourth Gospel.*

from them the impression of the Person and Character of Jesus of Nazareth, in its many-sided presentation. For me, the result upon the soul is that they place before me, in their picture of Him, an Object which the writers were evidently and altogether incapable of inventing in its mysterious, majestic, tender, holy greatness, and which again cannot reasonably be thought to have grown, as myth, out of the common workings of thought and belief in the relatively short time which sceptical criticism itself has to recognize as alone allowable before even the Fourth Gospel was written. The inference appears to me to be sound that that Object was not conceived or developed by the human mind but presented historically to it as absolute reality. In other words, Jesus of Nazareth, as Son of God, Son of Man, Sacrifice for sins, Lord of Resurrection, Friend of sinners, King of Glory, is fact. That being so I, for my part, take it to be reasonable to infer that the narratives to which alone, practically, I owe my sight of

Preliminaries

this altogether unique and absolutely pure
and great Phenomenon, the 'unspeakable
gift' of Heaven, are more than common
narratives. As common narratives I have
questioned them, and as such they deliver to
me a revelation which is itself enough to assure
me that the literary ground on which I am
admitted to behold it is holy ground. And
so I examine the Gospel, for example, of St
John with the conviction that I am meant
to read it as a holy thing, holy with a holiness profoundly akin to its topic. I read it
as a record 'caused to be written for my Rom. xv.
teaching' in such a sense that it is 'the 4
record which God hath given of His Son.' 1 John v.
10

Such a faith leaves unanswered, and without the least anxiety, very many questions
on which strictly literary investigation may
quite legitimately enter. For example, it
does not of itself tell me in what language,
Aramaic or Greek, the Lord's High Priestly
Prayer was actually uttered. It does not
even assure me that precisely those syllables,
no less, no more, no otherwise in any detail,

came as sounds from His lips that night. But it does assure me that in the record as it stands I have a report revised by the ever-blessed Speaker. It conveys to me absolutely, as it lies before me, lighted up by His Spirit, the mind of Jesus as He spoke that night to His Father, in the midst of the Eleven, lifting up His eyes to Heaven.

So, after this brief prelude, upon our attitude, and upon the simplicity of our method, let us approach the chapter and in detail consider it. And 'the Prayer of King Edward the Sixth' shall be ours as we do so :—

'O gracious God and most mercifull Father, which hast vouchsafed us the rich and precious jewell of Thy holy worde, assist us with Thy Spirit, that it may be written in our hearts to our everlasting comfort, to reforme us, to renew us according to Thine owne image, to build us up and edifie us into the perfect building of Thy Christ, sanctifying, and increasing in us all heavenly vertues. Graunt this, O heavenly Father, for Jesus Christes sake. Amen.'

II

Jesus Christ at Prayer

'These things spoke Jesus, and, lifting up His eyes to the heaven, said, Father, the hour is come; glorify Thy Son, that Thy Son may glorify Thee.'—JOHN xvii. 1.

So does the great High Priest begin His intercession. He has now 'spoken the things' of the previous chapters, 'the things concerning Himself,' and concerning His Father, and the Comforter, and the disciple's life in the living Vine, and his sight of the self-revealing Companion of his soul, and his possession of the Christ-glorifying Spirit. At length He has closed with the warning of tribulation and with the promise of peace, peace in Him the Overcomer. Now, already in the open air —for the 'eyes lifted up *to the heaven*' reasonably intimate that it was so—in the light of the Paschal moon, ready to cross the brook, He prays. Teachings, warnings, promises, revelations, lead up to prayer ; prayer carries them up to the throne ; they are ushered into the Holy Place, where the Father listens to the Son.

One inestimable treasure we have here already in this great Orison of the Lord, the treasure of a supreme example and encouragement to pray, to pray for others and for ourselves, to speak in simplicity to the Invisible God, to tell out our desires, across all mystery, to Him. We need that example always more and more. Who does not feel how that old tendency of the world, 'by wisdom not to know God'—at least, not to know Him as the living answerer of prayer—is stronger than ever in our day ? And our own sinful hearts will only too readily second the expressed or implied incredulity around us. Now one great antidote to a prayerless slumber on the Enchanted Ground is to read again the Scripture records of prayer, and above all of our Master's prayers. Within sound of the praying voice of Jesus the infidel misgiving will expire and the

1 Cor. i. 21

16

Jesus Christ at Prayer

Christian will recover his first simplicity.
When Jesus, the Jesus of this great Gospel,
He who has approved Himself to the soul as
the veritable 'Son of God, with power,' lifts up _{Rom. i. 4}
His eyes to the heaven, the Christian is thank-
ful to look thither also, with the simplicity
of a child, believing with a happy repose
of thought that 'beyond, beyond this lower
sky' shines the radiant reality of the heaven
of the immediate, blissful, all-loving Presence,
'the high and holy place.' When 'this same Isa. lvii.
Jesus,' looking up thither, *speaks*, the Christian ¹⁵
thankfully knows and owns, in deepest re-
assurance, that the utterances of human lips
are no vanity, no thing of nought, in that
region, to that supreme Personality; the
expression of our longings, the explanation
of our fears, the confession of our sins, is
what God looks for and approves. When
Jesus says 'Father,' and the Christian stands
by His side and listens, then across a thousand subtleties and sophisms, nay, amidst
innumerable mysteries impervious to his in-
tellect, baffling the finite mind as it attempts

to comprehend fully its own relations with the Infinite, he knows that the Eternal and Ultimate is Personal. The poor sinful man, looking up into the heights immeasurable, finds and touches, with trembling but real faith, close beside him, no mere abstract Cause, no blind Tendency, no soulless Nature personified and deified by fancy or by wish, but One who knows, wills, and loves, unspeakably and with a tenderness that cannot be imagined. He is the personally Holy, the personally Faithful, the personally Gracious. He is the Father, nothing less than all that can be denoted or implied by that dear and living word; the Father, first of our Lord Jesus Christ, and then of the praying, needing man in Him. He is Father, for He is living Author of our personal life; Father, for our very nature was made in His image; Father, 1 Pet. i. 3 for He has 'begotten us again unto a living hope.' He is Father, so that we are to Him immeasurably more than even the work of His hands: we are, to that eternal Love, His dear and precious possession; His 'delights are with the sons of men'; He 'pities' the Prov. viii. child of His mortal family with that 'pity' 3 Psa. ciii. of which only parental hearts can quite 13 know the sweet nature—the pity which is the outcome of a yearning affection, attracted by the very frailty of its object, and which also returns continually into that affection to quicken and kindle it yet more than ever. Listening to his Lord thus speaking, thus saying 'Father,' 'Holy Father,' 'Righteous Father,' 'Thou lovedst Me,' 'I have known Thee,' the man takes the great but perhaps almost too familiarly-known word up again, to study, and adore, and love. 'Our Father which art in heaven,' the first words of the first Lord's Prayer, are lighted up into a new and tender glory by these first words of this wonderful last Lord's Prayer; and the man says his *Pater Noster* as one who knows and feels that he can never be an orphan. Life may move on to its end ; he may experience with a haunting and indescribable sadness in himself what all too indifferently, perhaps, he has long seen in others, the inexorable deepening of life's solitudes, by bereavements, by alienations, by the numberless 'changes and decays' which the mere 'process of the suns' must bring, not least in a time of altogether abnormal alteration like our own.   But he who 2 John 9 'has the Father and the Son,'[1] the Father 1 John iv. in the Son, he who 'knows and believes the 16 love of God' to the 'many brethren' of His Rom. viii. Firstborn, this man lives to the very last in a 29 home, in a circle of supreme family love, which can never break up. So to the very last, keeping close to the Lord Jesus, the heart of the loved and loving child of the hearth-side shall be his.

And when he listens on, and hears Jesus speaking to that Father, and calling Himself His Son, and calling on Him to glorify His Son ; when he hears Him say, just later, that He was dear to that Father 'before the foundation of the world,' then with renewed thankfulness does the anxious heart address

---

[1] 'Who hath the Father and the Son
May be left, but not alone.'
                    Christian Year.

itself to pray, recognizing afresh not only
that 'God is,' but that He *must delight* to be
approached as the Father of this wonderful
Son, 'the Son of His love,' the Lord of our Col. i. 13
love.

So let us learn from our chapter at least
this—to pray. Because of the High Priestly
Prayer let us pray—more simply, more gladly,
speaking out our desires as to the living God,
as to our Father, as to the Father of our
Lord Jesus Christ. Yes, let us get to know
Him in prayer better and yet better as the
Father of our Lord. Let that name illuminate
the fathomless void of our ignorance, and let
it glorify all that we can call our knowledge.
To us also, O Lord our Father, let Thy Son
glorify Thee.

III

The Father, the Hour, the Glory

'Father, the hour is come; glorify Thy Son.'—
JOHN xvii. 1.

SO the Lord began to pray. 'FATHER';
such is the simplicity and sublimity
of His address; six times in this heavenly
prayer He uses the word. As we listen,
let us remember first His own earlier
Matt. xi. saying, 'No one knoweth the Father but
27 the Son, and he to whom the Son wills
to reveal Him'; and let us draw nearer
that the Son may do so, shewing Him to
us as indeed 'our Father.' If we would
realize to the full that wonderful relation-
ship, let us learn to view Him before all
as the Father of our Lord. Never shall
we exhaust the truth and joy hidden in
the Sonship of our Saviour. Never shall
we come to the end of its meaning as to

His own Godhead. And never shall we
come to the end of our own comfort in it
in view of that sonship 'by adoption and
grace' which is ours 'by faith in the Son
of God,' and of which the sweet, profound
expression, the voice in us of 'the Spirit
of the Son,' is the cry, 'Abba, Father.' Gal. iv. 6
Never let us deny the revelation of a
universal divine Fatherhood, affecting man
as man. But what assuredly is much more
prominent in Scripture, because much more
needful for some of the deepest needs of the
awakened soul, is that special Fatherhood
whose spiritual secret lies wholly in the Son,
and which is received in actual possession
and fruition by heaven-taught faith in Him.
'As many as received Him, to them gave John i. 12
He authority to become children of God.'
'As many as are led by the Spirit of God Rom. viii.
they are the sons of God.' 'Behold what 14 i John iii. 1
manner of love the Father hath bestowed
upon us that we should be called children
of God.'

So the believer listens with more than

even reverence as his Redeemer says
'FATHER.' The word is infinitely important to his heart. It is his own assurance
of a true sonship in the Son, real, sanctifying, gladdening for ever. He hears in it
Eph. i. 6 his own 'acceptance in the Beloved.'

'*The hour is come.*' Similar phrases to
this are frequent in the Gospels, and not
least in St John, and almost always they
refer to the Lord's saving work in one
phase of it or another. And the use of
these phrases is restricted very much to
Matt. the time of the Passion : 'Sleep on now;
xxvi. 45
Mark the hour is come'; 'Let this hour pass
xiv. 35
Luke from me'; 'This is your hour.' In St
xxii. 53
John the main instances are, 'They sought
vii. 30 to take Him, but no man laid hands on
Him, for His hour was not yet come';
viii. 20 'These words He spoke in the treasury;
xii. 23 and no man laid hands on Him, for His
xii. 27
hour was not come'; 'The hour is come
that the Son of Man should be glorified';
and then, immediately, just after that deep
word about the 'corn of wheat,' 'Father, save

24

The Father, the Hour, the Glory

Me from this hour: but for this cause came
I to this hour.' One more example meets
us in the narrative of the paschal night;
'Jesus knew that the hour had come that John
He should depart out of this world to the xiii. 1
Father.'

This collection, as we weigh its import
as a whole, may amply convince us that
the word 'hour' is used throughout in its
deepest significance. It means not merely
a crisis, or a fit time; it takes us round to
the unseen and eternal side of things, to
the time forewilled, the hour set down in
the divine counsels, in the faultless and
unrevealed wisdom of God, for the sacrifice
of His Christ. That 'fulness of the time,' Gal. iv. 4
even in its details, had been ordained from
an eternal point of vision. Its working out
into fact was perfectly harmonized, God
knows how, with the entirely natural play
of circumstances and with the living will of
man. But none the less it was a matter
of supreme and hidden *fiat*. The hour had
not come—and Jesus was left untouched.

The High Priestly Prayer

It struck — and He was betrayed and crucified.

And now, this long-purposed hour of glory and of agony Jesus recognizes, and John xii. accepts. Once at least already He has 27 shrunk from it in His holy and infinitely sensitive Manhood; and that very night, in the Garden, He is to feel the horror of it Heb. xii. *almost* over-balance 'the joy set before 2 Him.' Yet here He accepts it. Looking in unclouded peace to His Father, fully in view of the Father's glory, and of His own, He speaks of it as of a painless triumph; He says, not, 'Pity, succour, sustain,' but, 'Glorify Thy Son.' And in that great word, 'glorify,' assuredly He includes not only the splendour of the Resurrection and the Ascension but the whole ineffable experience before Him, the Garden, the Cross, and then the Rising from the grave and to the heavens; for it was all one thing. The 'glory' of the Son of God, for ever, in the world of glory, will reside in His being the Saviour while also the Son. Then,

The Father, the Hour, the Glory

did not *all* that constituted Him the perfect
Saviour, contribute to His glorification?   We
who believe in Him resolve, and rightly, 'not Gal. vi. 14
to glory save in His Cross'   To us the Cross
is essential to His holy dignity; He would
not be to us the adorable King that He
is but for that shame and agony through
which in the majesty of His mercy He
went for us.   Well has Vinet sung of the
Victim upon the Cross:—

> ' To Thy immortal forehead bright
>   A mould as heavenly here is given
> As ever in the sacred light,
>   As ever in the calm of heaven ;
> Never in beauty's native home
>   So vivid was Thy beauty's glow
> As when, to-day, in solemn gloom
>   Up Calvary Thy feet must go.' [1]

So I presume to see involved in the
words 'Glorify Thy Son' the whole process
of the Passion and the Victory; they include
the sweat of blood, and the mysterious *Lama*

---

[1] I quote from a translation by my brother of A. Vinet's
magnificent hymn, *Sous Ton voile d'ignominie.*   The translation (signed ' C. W. M.') is printed in Archdeacon Moule's
Songs of Heaven and Home, p. 141, ed. 1905.

heard from the darkness over the Cross. The glory He requests is that which through eternity will mark Him as 'the Lamb that was slain.' 'Crown Me with My atoning death. Let Me become glorious in Thy sight, and in the sight of My redeemed in all ages, and for ever, as Him who died, the Sacrifice. Give Me the cup of trembling, that I may become eternally the cause, and the means, between them and Thee, of peace and life.'

As we close our short contemplation, we note in the very prayer, 'Glorify Thou Me,' an implication of the Deity of Him who utters it. What creature, however exalted, could so call upon the Majesty on high? It is the voice of the Son, but of GOD the Son.

On the other hand, it is the voice of God, but of God the SON. He who speaks addresses One whom He delights to reveal as the eternal Fountain of Himself the Eternal Stream; who Himself so loved the world that He gave His Son; who is to be measured in His measureless glory and

The Father, the Hour, the Glory

goodness by the thought that He is the Father of the SON; and on whom that Son, infinite and co-equal in His Nature, yet looks as alone able, because of His Fatherhood, to crown Him with glory.

IV

The Gift given to the Son

'That Thy Son also may glorify Thee: as Thou hast given Him power over all flesh, that He should give eternal life to as many as Thou hast given Him.'—JOHN xvii. 1, 2.

'*THAT Thy Son also may glorify Thee.*'
This is the ultimate aim of the great
Phil. ii. 2 Intercessor—the glory of His Father; 'that every tongue may confess that Jesus Christ is Lord, *to the glory of God the Father*'; that the redeemed and renewed, in their ever-growing hosts, may say, with 'the Spirit of
2 Cor. i. His Son' in their hearts, 'Blessed be the God
3, etc. and Father of our Lord Jesus Christ.' Let us seek for a deeper apprehension always of the absolute unity of will and love between the Giver and the Son whom He gave. We believe and receive the love of Christ; we penetrate, if I may say so, into its sacred depth—and we find no breach of continuity behind it; no colder region, as if the Father

were less tender than the Son. The love is 'the love of God, which is in Jesus Christ our Lord.' Rom. v. 39

Ver. 2. '*Even as Thou gavest Him authority over all flesh, so that as to the whole which Thou hast given Him He may give to them life eternal.*'

'*Even as*' denotes a close connexion of cause and purpose, and the connexion appears to be somewhat thus:—'That Thy Son may glorify Thee, especially in the salvation of men, which salvation consists in their knowing Thee in Him and Him in Thee. Let Me thus glorify Thee, for Thou gavest Me My mission for that very end. Bear Me victorious through My sacrificial work, and this will be according to Thy will that men should be drawn in Me to Thee.'

'*Thou gavest Him authority over all flesh*'; over humanity, over man as man; a giving which surely dates from before (or let us say, above) all measured time; an eternal grant and compact, if such words current in the transactions of our finite life may be humbly used to help thought a little here. Paternal Deity gave and Filial Deity received that fore-ordered office and operation; and it was so, on purpose that the grant of life eternal might be brought to 'the whole which Thou hast given Him.'

In these last words, as we read them under recollection of a large mass of other Scriptures, we can hardly doubt that there lies before us the mystery, 'dark with excess of bright,' of a divine election. Very reverently and very briefly I presume to speak here of this great matter: Eccl. v. 2 'God is in heaven and we on earth; therefore let our words be few.' At the very utmost, from our mortal point of view, and finite as we are, we can see very little of its scope. No graver mistake can thought make than to treat it as if we knew all, and to build a full-orbed system upon such fancied knowledge. For myself, a very few steps of meditation into the theme of the election of God are enough to bring the soul to a pause, first to adore His unsearchableness, then to embrace with the very simplest faith the Cross of Him who

The Gift given to the Son

died for all, then, kneeling there, at rest before the Crucified, to realize that we know enough, seeing His 'sacred head once wounded,' to trust His Father altogether with what we do not know.

Some short detached remarks will be sufficient here.

i. The Biblical phrases about the election of God almost invariably, in their large variety, are used as of a deep and holy *mystery*. Whatever it is, its origin is in eternity, and its goal is holiness and glory. And again, it is emphatically presented as something which is 'not according to our 2 Tim. i. 9 works'; in other words, as ruled by reasons which are reasons indeed, radiant with truth and love, but—for the present however— beyond our reach.

ii. The scope of the election and 'gift' looks, it would appear, beyond time into eternity. Two adjacent sentences in St John, whose writings even more than St Paul's are our main guide here, seem to make this clear: 'The whole which the Father giveth

John vi. 37, 39 Me shall come to Me'; 'This is the Father's will, that, as to the whole which He hath given Me, I should lose nothing out of it, but should raise it up in the last day.'

iii. On the other hand we remember quite as distinctly the limitations placed by Scripture itself on this deep element of revelation. In the first place it is brought up but seldom in comparison with the abundant and glowing utterances, spoken without reserve or drawback, about the Saviour's sacrifice, and 1 John ii. 2 about His invitation. He is 'the propitiation for the sins of the whole world'; God, in Him, 1 Tim. ii. 4 'willeth all men to be saved.' Again, it is almost always presented not as a mystery placed in a formidable prominence at the threshold of the Gospel, but as a secret of its inner and most tranquil sanctuary. It is a matter for which *the believer* is to be prepared, so far as it is indicated to his thought, by what else and otherwise he knows of the love and faithfulness of the Eternal; it is to be handled aright by those only who have come to know God as the Father,

The Gift given to the Son

infinitely good, whom they can safely trust with many things past finding out. Again, it is never fatalistically presented in the Bible, no, not for a moment ; it is indissolubly bound up with the personal will of Him who is love. And yet again, it is always practically set forth in the Bible ; it is a choice and call, however it acts, and wherever it acts, to kindness, humbleness, meekness, longsuffering, love. Lastly, it is never so shewn to us as to deter or discourage one single soul which asks for light and life. It is shown so as to humble man into a profound sense of his finite insight into the methods of the Infinite, but at the same moment so as to encourage, not the secure but the wistful disciple, with the thought of an embrace which, unspeakably unworthy as he is, will certainly not lightly leave him nor soon forsake him.

As we close, let us thankfully remember how, as a fact, the most divergent views of this great secret have not forbidden servants and saints of God to experience a like rejoicing in their Saviour. And then let us

The High Priestly Prayer

turn back once more, with peace and with thanksgiving, to the verse which has suggested to our thoughts these few words upon a deep problem of the faith. Let us read in that verse, as if for the first time, the assurance that the Lord Jesus has received eternal 'authority' to give to us sinful men the very life eternal, and that He delights to give it. Let us recollect afresh that we deal, in our supplications for that life, not with an impersonal law but with supreme Love incarnate, with Him who says perpetually, not in the Isa. xlv. light only but also in the darkness, 'Look 22; Matt xi unto Me and be saved ; Come unto Me and I 28 will give you rest.'

> 'Just as I am, without one plea
> But that Thy blood was shed for me,
> And that Thou bidd'st me come to Thee,
> O Lamb of God, I come.'

V

The Finished Work

'I glorified Thee on the earth; I finished the work which Thou gavest Me to do.'—JOHN xvii. 4.

SUCH is the Lord's summary of what He did 'in the days of His flesh'; this is His view of Birth, Childhood, Miracles, Discourses, Death and Resurrection; for here most surely He includes the Passion and its sequel, in this wonderful anticipatory *past tense*. What was the issue of it all? It was this; 'I glorified Thee.' To manifest the Father's love, to magnify His law, to show men what the Father really is by presenting Himself before them as the Father's Son, this was the ultimate aim of all that Jesus was, and worked, and bore. He came to be one with us, and He gave Himself for us, that we sinners might know with joy what we were doing when we should say, full in view of our own unspeakable demerit, but looking unto Jesus, 'ABBA, FATHER.'

Meantime, from this very summing-up of His ministry as one long glorification of the Father, let us gather tokens also of His own glory. Very largely the work was done by glorifying Himself, by testifying to Himself, as the Object of the sinful soul's absolute trust and love. What theory of the Person of Jesus except that of the Nicene Creed really answers to this wonderful phenomenon? He who thus glorifies the Eternal by presenting Himself as His Likeness must be indeed GOD the SON.

'*I finished the work which Thou gavest Me to do.*' So did He preface the prayer, 'Now glorify Thou Me.' For our Leader, the Crown was indeed preluded by the Cross; **Heb. xii. 1** first the 'finished work,' then 'the joy set before Him.' Shall not we strive, at our infinite distance, to follow Him here? We will not indolently pine for a state where conflict will be over just because we would

38

The Finished Work

fain shun the conflicts which await us here; we will not ask for rest and bliss above because we have no heart for the work of our King below. Nor again, if true to Him, will we choose and pick our service, giving it *to ourselves* to do; for the self-selected task may mean the neglect of precisely that work which the Father has actually given us. We will be willing for labours much less inviting, and, what is harder, much less fruitful, to all appearance, than those which, by a little trifling with the true call, we may shape out for ourselves. We will remember that our dear Lord's own 'finished work' seemed, in outward show, not greatly fruitful when it closed. One malefactor's rescued spirit was carried with Him into glory; a few timid friends just dared to bury His sacred body; about five hundred people, a congregation 1 Cor. xv. for one modest modern church, were the 6 largest company that ever gathered to look upon His risen form and to hear His great commission. But the work was the Father's gift, and as such it was duly finished; and then within a little while it burst into fruitfulness indeed; it bore fruit that 'shall remain' till the day when the countless nations of the Blessed shall all and for ever know that their heaven is the effect of that once seeming failure, the shedding of the blood of the Lamb.

> 'Come, Lord, when grace hath made me meet
>   Thy blessed face to see ;
> *For if Thy work on earth be sweet*
>   What will Thy glory be ?'

Ver. 5. *And now glorify Thou Me, Father, by Thine own side, with the glory which I had before the universe was, by Thy side.*

'*I* glorified Thee ; do *Thou* Thy part now for Me'; such is the emphasis and balance of the sentences. And again we ask, as we listen and worship, who could claim this reciprocity but God the Son of God ?

'*By Thy side* ;' such undoubtedly is the sense of the Greek. The 'with Thine own self,' 'with Thee,' of the Authorized Version is at the best indistinct as a translation. The thought is of place and position, if we

The Finished Work

may use such words to shape and define our
thought a little.   He means 'the right hand Heb. viii.
of the throne of the majesty in the heavens'; ¹
He is in thought where Stephen saw Him,
'standing at the right hand of God.' The Acts vii.
same glorious aspect of things appears in the ⁵⁵
first words of this Gospel; 'the Word was John i. 1
face to face with God' (so we presume to
paraphrase, in order to bring out the force of
the preposition in the original), in the eternal
intimacy of the Throne.

These are strange utterances to come from
human lips.   And yet they did so come,
from lips which within twenty-two hours
were to be as cold and rigid as ours one day
will be when the last sigh is gone.   What
shall we think of the words?   Surely, that
they mean either Deity, Filial Diety—or mad-
ness.   And we need not tremble over the
alternative, when, in the photograph of the
Gospels, we look not at the lips only but at
the face.   Lord Jesus Christ, we see Thee,
and we believe.   We believe that thou wast
before the worlds; that Thou wast born in

the world; that Thou art the Son of the Father; that Thou art the Son of Man, the Mother's Son; of one essence with God; of one essence with us; the Christ of all our hopes, and of all our desires, and of all our love.

'*At Thine own side.*' We cannot pierce more than a step at the most into the *local* form of the wonderful phrase. The *moral* meaning is clear; the Incarnate Son looks to be lifted in His Incarnation to universal empire, beside Him who sent Him. And the very fact that He is the Incarnate emboldens us to think, with reverence, of His ' session' as in some sort locally conditioned; for surely *somewhere* in the glorious unseen is the sacred transfigured body which went up from the hill above Jerusalem. But we need not say more, we hardly need think more, in that direction. It shall be amply enough for faith and love, as they listen at the curtains of eternity, to recollect that the darkness there—as it seems to us now to be—will be seen by us one day lighted up in its whole

The Finished Work

boundless sphere by the fact that at its centre, 'by the side of' the Father, lives the Son, our Brother and our Head.

Safe region, and happy, for those who are found in Him!

> 'Beyond that welcome door
> I know, (and oh for more
>   Why should I care?)
> I shall my Saviour see
> As now He seeth me;
>   Jesus is there.'

'C. W. B.,' *On the Death of the Rev. J. W. Birch.*
—*Evening Hours*, June 1872.   See note, p. 221.

VI

Glorification : Manifestation

'Glorify Thou Me, by Thine own side, with the glory which I had, before the universe was, by Thy side.'—JOHN xvii. 5.

I VENTURE to paraphrase somewhat thus : 'Give Me now that exaltation in My Human Nature which is Mine eternally in My Divine Nature; let Me be "*the Son of Man* at the right hand of God," upon "the throne of God *and of the Lamb*."'

Acts vii. 56; Rev. xxii. 1

To such an interpretation we are helped upward by many other Scriptures. When we explain otherwise we are soon lost in mystery; for who can say for certain that the humiliation of the Lord during His life on earth did, or did not, involve an abeyance of His divine glory in the Holy Place? And who then can say that there was, or was not, occasion, when He ascended, for the

restoration of the 'effulgence' of that glory? Heb. i. 3
Silence is our best tribute before such a
secret; whereas it is evident that when this
Prayer was spoken He had not yet as the
Incarnate and Crucified been raised to
heaven; not yet had the enthronement
figured out in Rev. v. taken place, when
'all the company of heaven,' and all the
heights and depths of created being, sung
their Hallelujah song to Him who had been
slain for our redemption. In respect of *that*
exaltation there was certainly room still, on
the Paschal night, for the prayer, 'Glorify
Me.' So He requests here to be thus 'glorified.' He asks for the 'joy and crown' of
being known directly to the heavenly host
and mediately to us below as the supreme
Conqueror through fellowship and sacrifice,
the 'Priest on His throne,' who reached that Zech. vi.
throne by way of being laid first, for us, upon 13
the altar. Such 'glory' is no cold or barren
éclat; it is a fame and greatness infinitely
moral, eternally beneficent; it is the splendour
of being known for ever as the Lord who

The High Priestly Prayer

Phil. ii.
4, 8 indeed 'looked not on His own things,' but
for the Father, and for us, 'obeyed, even unto
death, even unto the Cross.'

But then, from another side, from the
eternal side, as regards *the Person* thus
glorified, in respect of the 'glory' being a
grandeur assigned to the SON—it is a glory
which was His 'before the universe was.'
Wonderful phrase; do not let it pass as if it
were too familiar for attention. Let us group
it with the many kindred Scripture words:
Col. i. 15,
17; Eph.
i. 4 'He is before all things'; 'The Firstborn
before all creation'; 'He chose us in Him
before the foundation of the world'; and
ver. 24 again below, 'Thou didst love Me before
the foundation of the world.' Think of the
awful, the unfathomable significance of such
phrases; view it for the moment in one light
only, the light of our constantly growing
knowledge of the antiquity of material
creation. Take only the regions of geo-
logical time, forgetting the incalculable
vastness of antecedent ages; think of what
someone has called the 'almost eternities'

of the Primary and Secondary Periods as they lie chronicled in the rocks. And then reflect that the Son, the Word, the Christ, He who for us became the Jesus of the Cradle and the Cross, was, or rather is, not only antecedent to all this but also its Cause; 'by Him, and for Him,' the Father 'made the æons.' Happy the student of Nature who can see the glory of his Saviour expand, as it were, with the ever-expanding wonder of the material universe. 'I will see Jesus,' said the dying Brewster, passing with joy from his 'knowledge in part' to the upper and more perfect light; 'I will see Jesus who made the worlds; and that will be grand.'

Col. i. 16; Heb. i. 2

Ver. 6. '*I did manifest Thy Name to the men whom Thou hast given Me out of the world. They were Thine, and to Me Thou hast given them, and Thy word they have kept.*'

Again, as in ver. 2, we have here intimated to us that 'deep thing of God,' a

divine choice, and a gift, by the Father to
the Son, 'out of the world.' All we will
remember about it further here is that it
is the lips of the Lord Jesus which speak
of it; and they who know Him can trust
Him with all secrets; secrets are safe with
Him till that coming hour when, so far as
the finite can learn from the Infinite without
John iv.25 reserve, 'He will tell us all things.' So considered, the words before us are full of help
to the believing soul. 'To those whom Thou
hast given Me *I did manifest* Thy Name.'
Have we in any measure known that manifestation? Then let us bless the Father and
the Son, and recognize in our own unworthy
hearts the touch of the eternal hands. Has
the light and sublime beauty of the Father
2 Cor. iv. been unveiled to us at all 'in the face of
6 Jesus Christ'? Have we seen in Him, as
souls see, not the First Cause only, or only
the King, or only the Judge, or only a
benignant Providence, or only an indulgent
'Good God'—but the FATHER, the Father
of the Only-begotten Son, and our veritable

Glorification : Manifestation

Father also, as we live in Christ and in Him also are the sons of God? Then let us reverently say, not in our own names but in His, that a great miracle has been wrought in us. The gift of the Father has embraced our sinful beings; the Son of the Father has come into contact with our wills, our affections, our reason, and has manifested to us the Name.

'*I manifested to them Thy Name.*' So He had done with that group of men around Him. They had not been wholly ignorant of it before; they had read in their Book of the Prophets that 'doubtless Thou art our Father.' But the older revelation shewed the glorious truth though the twilight only, and they, Peter, John, James, and the rest, had seen it but partially even so. Aye, and up to that very hour they held their partial knowledge with very feeble hands; for think what miseries of doubt and even of despair they were to encounter in the actual sight of the Cross next day. Nevertheless already, in knowing the SON, in some genuine measure, Isa. lxiii. 16; lxiv. 8

49

they knew, *in principle*, immeasurably more of the Name of the FATHER than could otherwise be known.

They could not have put their knowledge into adequate expression. The day would come when they should do so; when Peter 1 Pet. i. 3 should write, 'Blessed be the God and Father of our Lord Jesus Christ,' and John should 1 John i. 3 write, 'Our fellowship is with the Father, and with His Son.' But this was not yet. They must first be more broken in themselves, and then they must be filled with the Spirit of the Son. Nevertheless, through whatever clouds, they had got a living glimpse of Heb. i. 3 JESUS. And Jesus is 'the express Image' of Him that sent Him.

VII

Divine Optimism

'And they have kept Thy word.'—JOHN xvii. 6.

So closes this pregnant sixth verse. We have noticed already, when thinking upon the words, 'I have manifested unto them Thy Name,' the Lord's gracious style of speech about the very imperfect reception by His disciples of His manifestation of the Name. They had seen only a glimpse of that Name by comparison with what they were yet to see; nevertheless He is pleased to speak of the glimpse as if it were the larger sight, for the larger sight lay latent in it as the flower lies in the bud.

The same most merciful and loving *optimism*, if I may use the term, appears in the clause now before us, and in a form still

more beautiful, if possible, than ever. Are
not these words a surprise to us, a spiritual
paradox, when we reflect upon some features
in the Gospel portrait of the Apostles?
Think of the moment when the Lord asked
how long He should suffer the faithlessness
and the perversity of their hearts; of the
moment when He turned upon their leader
and said, 'Get thee behind Me, Satan, for
thou savourest not the things of God.'
Remember them at the time when they
shewed how little they had understood the
full issues of the Father's 'word' as it was to
produce a life of holy love—when they
pressed the Lord to get rid of the trouble-
some Syrophœnician mother, and tried to
prevent the poor little children from 'coming
to His arms to be blest.' Look at them as
they 'disputed among themselves' upon the
road, which was to be the greatest personage
in the coming kingdom, and again when they
'forbade' the man who was casting out the
devils in their Lord's Name, because he would
not acknowledge them as the only true

Matt.
xvi. 23;
xvii. 17

Matt. xv.
27; Mark
ix. 34, 38;
Luke
xviii. 15

Divine Optimism

representatives of Messiah. Let us indeed think every such thought with all humble reverence towards the holy Apostles as we see them in the light which grace and providence finally threw around them. And let us never for a moment forget that every iota of our acquaintance with their weaknesses of insight, of temper, of act and word, all we know of their complaints and objections, their ambitions and jealousies, is given to us through *their own* nobly truthful account of themselves; for whatever the problems may be which gather round the structure of the four Gospels, their narratives, their portraits, are ultimately apostolic ; and no deeper evidence to their pure veracity can be afforded than what we have in these unflattering portraits of their originators. But when we have remembered all this, the wonder still remains, in view of these portraits, that the Lord Jesus, just then and there, should have said of them, looking up to His Father, 'They have kept Thy word.'

Yet, when we think more closely and

deliberately, is not the wonder itself only another note of truth? For is not this gracious optimism, if I may once more presume to call it so, this delight to see the best, to single out for praise all that was in the least degree praiseworthy, as deeply true to the mysterious perfectness of the Lord's character as the shortcomings of the Apostles are true to the limitations of their sinful humanity? It has been observed from very old times that the nobler a heart is the more it loves to praise. It is, I think, a critic of antiquity (is it not Aristotle himself?) who finds one note of the surpassing greatness of Homer in the pervading accents of admiration and applause with which he celebrates his heroes; the exact opposite in this respect to the satirist who seizes the weaker, the baser side, and lays his emphasis there. And 'a greater than Homer is here.' And He, true to His sacred character, which is love, takes up the imperfect but genuine welcome which these men have given to His message, and makes the most of it. He

Divine Optimism

thinks of them as those who 'forsook all and followed Him,' for His word's sake. He remembers how one of them had said, treading his own prejudices underfoot, 'Rabbi, Thou art the Son of God'; how another had said, when great groups of people were giving Him up altogether as their teacher and leader, 'Lord, to whom else shall we go? Thou hast the words of eternal life.' He sees a present beauty in all these actual confessions, and He looks forward, even across the terrible failure they were all about to make that very night, and of which He forewarned them, to the fast approaching days when they, trained by Him and filled with His Spirit, should not only 'keep the Father's word' but teach the world how to keep it.

Such an utterance is indeed characteristic of the Lord. Who has not read that beautiful legend of Nazareth, preserved, I believe, in Persian literature, which tells us of the poor dead dog cast out into the street and noticed with only loathing looks and

Luke v. 11

John i. 49

John vi. 68

words by the passers-by? But the Son of
the Carpenter came walking that way in His
turn, and gazed upon the repellent sight.
And then He said, 'Pearls are not whiter
than its teeth!'

The spirit of those words is present, in a
far deeper and loftier connexion indeed, but
the same, in these. And it speaks again and
again, as we shall amply hear—it speaks in
even sublimer accents—in later passages of
the Prayer.

Let us close with the simple but all-
precious, all-encouraging recollection that the
heart which thus beat with a gracious
'optimism' that night, in the High-priestly
intercession, is 'the same yesterday, and to-
day, and for ever.' To-day, this hour, we
His unworthy followers, His slow-hearted
disciples, we who so much mistake Him, so
feebly trust Him, so faintly love Him, have
yet to do with 'this same Jesus.' He is
able this hour not only 'to be touched
with a feeling of our infirmities,' but to
look through the golden light of His

Heb. xiii. 8

Heb. iv. 15

Divine Optimism

wonderful love upon the poor imperfect efforts of our souls to keep His word and to follow Him. Let it abase us to the dust. Let it uplift us to a conscious nearness to His heart.

VIII

The Father and the Son

'Now have they come to understand that all things whatsoever Thou hast given Me are from Thee; because the sayings which Thou gavest Me I have given them; and they received them, and recognized truly that from beside Thee I came out, and believed that Thou didst send Me.'—JOHN xvii. 7, 8.

WE have here an expansion of the sentence just above, 'I manifested to them Thy Name.' The burthen of the words before us is this throughout: the Father glorified in the Son, the Son the Revealer of the Father.

'*They have come to understand*'; so I render the Greek, in view of the verb chosen, and of the perfect tense. It denotes an arrival through sight at recognition; a certain attained insight, a seeing into the significance of a glorious phenomenon. Such was in fact their privilege

58

The Father and the Son

and attitude, in the grace of God; always with the limitations which we noticed in the previous reading, and always with the remembrance of that most generous *optimism* of their Lord's view of them of which also we took account.

'*That all things whatsoever Thou hast given Me are from Thee.*' There is no tautology here. The Lord refers to a 'gift' of 'things' to Him, as to a matter of His own absolute knowledge, and then to the fact that His disciples had recognized those 'things' as such, had seen them to be the gifts of the Father to the Son. These 'things' appear clearly, in the light of ver. 9, to be the message, the commission, which He bore as Saviour and as Prophet; the 'sayings' of life and light eternal which He had brought from the bosom of the Father, and which were embodied into a glorious and saving potency in His Person and His Work. Such 'sayings' are before us here as, for example, that preserved in John iii. 16, or again in vi. 40, with their mighty revelation of sinful man's title, in the Only Son, on terms of simple and submissive faith, to a welcome into the very embrace and heart of the Supreme Love. Such 'sayings' as those which tell our wistful souls that the Son came not to judge the world, but to save it; that 'verily, verily, he that believeth on the Son, relieth on the Son, hath eternal life, and shall not come into judgement, but hath passed over from the death unto the life'; that 'he that eateth the Son shall live on account of Him,' and 'shall be raised up by Him at the last day'; that 'if any man serve the Son him will the Father honour'; that 'the Father Himself loveth' those who 'have loved the Son and have believed that He came forth from God'; yea, that to such as 'keep the word of the Son' the Father and the Son 'will come, and make Their abode with them'—these and such like are the 'sayings' in question here.

Two great saving messages emerge from

John v. 24; vi. 39, 57; xii. 26, 47; xiv. 23; xvi. 27

60

The Father and the Son

even the briefest view of such 'sayings' so referred to here by the Lord. The first is the glory of the Father, the second is the glory of the Son.

i. The glory of the Father. Behold HIM here presented to us by the Lord Jesus as the original and unfathomable Fountain of redeeming love. It comes supremely of the Father's goodness, and thought, and will, that the world of sinful humanity should have a Saviour, that that world, man by man, should be called to receive in Him all that God means by eternal life, that believing man, simply as such, in the Son, should not perish, but should have that life for ever, and be raised up at the last day, and be with the Only Begotten everlastingly where He is. Here is the warrant of Him who alone absolutely 'knows the Father' that the human soul Matt. xi. 27 cannot look with too perfect a confidence, with a trust too happy and artless, in the intercourse of love and prayer, to the 'blessed God and Father of our Lord 2 Cor. i. 3

The High Priestly Prayer

Jesus Christ.' In Him, as here we amply understand, is no half-averted Power, no almost hostile Deity. He is the Giver of Rom. xi. our Lord Jesus Christ, out of 'the depth 33 of the riches' of His wisdom and His love, a depth stirred to its wonderful overflow only and solely by His own Nature, by His sacred Self, yearning over the creature whom He has made, and whom He re-makes, for His delight, in His Incarnate Son. Let Vinet sing our thoughts about this:

> ' The Father's word was, *I am Love;*
> Then Jesus left the home on high,
> To make this earth the message prove—
> *I am His Son, and Love am I.*'[1]

To hear the Son is to hear the Father; to see the Son is to see the Father; to be safe in the Son is to be safe in the very Col. iii. 3 shrine of the Father's love; 'your life is hid, with Christ, in GOD.'

ii. On the other hand, for it is always a balance and interaction of glorious truths

---

[1] See note, p. 27.

The Father and the Son

which meets us when we contemplate the
revelation of our God, we find here, as we
found under other words earlier in the
Prayer, that with each access of praise
and glory to the Father there rises also,
ever higher, the praise and glory of the
Son. We observed before that Jesus our
Lord glorifies the Father above all by
glorifying Himself as our hope and life.
In the chain of brief quotations which we
linked together just now this must have
come home to us. There always the
supreme proof of the Father's greatness
and goodness is the SON. The highest
will of the Father is that we should
believe on the SON. The Son speaks
indeed as being His Father's Servant,
His Messenger, as doing His commissioned
work. But always there is an undertone
which implies immeasurably more also at
the basis of it all. It is the voice of One
whose mission is from a height above all
finite and temporal being; who came from,
and returns to, the level of nothing less

than the Throne of all things; whom man can never trust too absolutely or love too wholly; One therefore who is God.

'Thou art the King of Glory, O Christ: Thou art the everlasting Son of the Father.' And the Christ accepts that homage; He knows Himself for the KING. Never does He so glorify His all-blessed Father as to withdraw Himself; never so as to intimate that in due time the disciple may learn to 'come to the Father' otherwise than 'by Him.' Here, under the very shadow of the close of His earthly witness, and more than ever, we find the very opposite to such a thought. The life eternal is, for ever, 'to know the only true God — and Jesus Christ whom He hath sent'; to whom He hath 'committed all things'—because He, co-essential, co-eternal, is capable of the commission.

IX

The Intercessor and His Own

'I pray for them : I pray not for the world, but for them which Thou hast given Me ; for they are Thine.'—JOHN xvii. 9.

THE seventh and eighth verses were last before us. As we leave them let us reflect upon the view they give us of the gladness of the Son of God in the thought that He has effectually revealed the Father to His disciples. And let us learn in our little measure to imitate our Master here. If His supreme desire was to set forth the glory of Him that sent Him, it shall be ours also, in every effort, large or small, for 'the testimony of His truth,' to make not ourselves but Him our beloved and absorbing object. Alas for us if it should be otherwise. The 'Christian work' which has, in any real sense, in the worker's thoughts, the worker for its centre, is a path to bitter disappointments at the best. But the work which in sincerity finds at once its motive and its goal in the Lord, because He is the Alpha and Omega of the worker's spirit, is the seed of harvests of pure and exceeding joy; yea, though it die, yet shall it live.

Ver. 9. 'I (the pronoun is emphatic) *am requesting about them. Not about the world am I requesting, but about those whom Thou hast given Me, because they are Thine.*'

'*I am requesting about them*;' 'requesting,' not 'enquiring'; the meaning here of the verb ($\dot{\epsilon}\rho\omega\tau\hat{a}\nu$) is settled by its use below in ver. 20. In classical Greek it means only and always 'to enquire'; in Biblical Greek it means also to 'request.' We observe further that its usage always, in Scripture, gives a dignity of its own to that meaning; the 'requesting' which it denotes is the asking not of an inferior, not of a suppliant, but of an equal; an asking supported and elevated by greatness and right. Never does the Saviour use the parallel verb ($a\dot{\iota}\tau\epsilon\hat{\iota}\nu$, $a\dot{\iota}\tau\epsilon\hat{\iota}\sigma\theta a\iota$) of His requests to His Father; and, on the other

The Intercessor and His Own

hand, there is no *certain* case of the employment of the verb used here where the prayer of mere man is in question; it appears to be consecrated to the desires and askings of our Lord. Thus the 'request' here stands on the same level with the 'will' of ver. 24. It lifts us to the thought of an advocacy which is great indeed. We hear in it the accent of a voice, speaking for us in the ears of supreme Holiness and Love, which is the voice of One whose place is not that of a suppliant before the throne but of its co-eternal Occupant. None less than HE says here, '*I* am requesting,' with an emphasis upon the 'I' which accentuates both His dignity and His free-will.

'*Not about the world*.' This most certainly does not mean that the Lord Jesus never 'requests' on 'the world's' behalf; only that He was not doing so then and there. Then and there, precisely at this moment of the intercession, He was keeping the faithful Apostles exclusively in view, as the context plainly indicates if we trace it down to ver. 20. As

The High Priestly Prayer

distinguished from that inmost circle, and for the purposes of this intercessory act, 'the world' of fallen humanity in general is put out of view, and the 'request' concentrates its sacred force upon a selected object.

Putting aside accordingly all questions about a world-wide advocacy on our Lord's part, let us now thankfully note the positive message of this verse, as of ver. 20 also with its vastly larger yet still selective scope. Here is an assurance that the Intercessor does make special request, in a sense unspeakably particular, for His own. That assurance is confirmed by most if not all of the other leading references to His work as our Friend on high; by the 'intercession made *for us*' of Rom. viii. 33; by the 'appearance in the presence of God *for us*' of Heb. ix. 24; by the '*we have* an Advocate with the Father' of 1 John ii. 1.

It is a side of truth which sometimes needs re-statement, this speciality of the Lord's regard and action. It is amply right, it is due to the glorious largeness of the Gospel, that we should very often indeed extol and bear witness to the pure, unbounded, 'philan- Tit. iii. 4 thropy' of our God, His love of man as man, His 'will that all men should be saved,' His 1 Tim. ii. sympathetic attention to the most inarticulate 4 of human needs and cries. But there are moments when the speciality of His love and of His promises is the very breath of life to the troubled disciple. It is the supreme need of the soul sometimes to say on the one hand, 'I know Him whom *I* have believed,' 2 Tim. i. and on the other hand to remember that 12 precisely for the believer, that is, for the sinner reliant on the accepted Christ, does He appear in the presence of God. 'For me, for me He careth, with an elder Brother's care,' for I, even I, am one of the family of faith, and therefore one of that Israel whose names are on His breastplate in the eternal See sanctuary. Exod. xxviii. 29

We have remembered that the Apostles were the precise objects before the mind of Jesus just then ; and He had, as we shall see further on, blessing after blessing to 'request' for them quite special to their case ; not till later does He pray for believers simply as believers. Yet we may rightly take, from this specimen of a particular intercession, the far-reaching comfort of the great fact that He who loves particularly prays particularly, whether for Apostle or for believer. And let us take that comfort heartily and without fear. Let us not too anxiously scrutinize the exact quality and quantity of our faith before we do so. Most certainly let us not ask for any special disclosure of the secrets of the divine will before we do so. Let us look unto Jesus, and in that look let us humbly find that He is our desire, our hope, our refuge, our Possessor; and let us remember that He never, never can despise the weakest reliance upon Him. Then, with a true humility, true because perfectly simple, for it is only the sight of our own entire and Eph. iii. absolute demerit, let us use the 'boldness' of 12 the Christian. Let us say, 'As sure as He is true to Himself, to His promises, to His work, to His character, He is true, in a wonderful particularity, to me. He knows and He

prays for me. Not for the world, in respect
of this inner relation and connexion, but for
me, He is making request. I will repose in
the special advocacy of my Lord for me.'

'Lord,' said an Apostle, a very little while
before this Prayer was spoken, 'how is it that John xiv.
Thou wilt manifest Thyself unto us and not ^{22, 23} unto the world?' 'If a man love Me he will
keep My words, and My Father will love *him*,
and We will come *unto him*, and make Our
abode *with him*.'

X

'Glorified in Them'

'And I have been glorified in them.'—JOHN xvii. 10.

THIS is a sentence most gracious and most
surprising. Not long ago, under ver. 6,
we had occasion to dwell on that *optimism*
of love with which our Lord regarded and
commended the spirit and experience of His
followers. That optimism, which appears
also in ver. 8, rises to its height in this brief
and wonderful affirmation from the lips of
the Son, speaking as if He were already on
the throne, our Advocate on high, in the
secret place of the Almighty. 'Glorified in
them'! Could it possibly be so indeed?
Could the radiance of His sacred beauty
and majesty, in any sense, and to any
observers, have been enhanced through
those Galileans, with their imperfect moral

development, their views of themselves and of their Lord so dim and inadequate, their very frequent mistakes of thought and failures of conduct? We recollect what we called up to view over that earlier passage; their partial insight, their earthly hopes, their narrowness of thought, their lack of sympathy with the needs of others, their doubts sometimes of their Master's ability and wisdom, their inability, even up to the resurrection morning, fully to understand His way of salvation. Yet somehow, wonderful as was the paradox, the fact was so, for He affirmed it; He *had* been glorified in them. In some opinion, before some observers, the Lord Jesus had actually received through them what He calls glory; the radiant virtue of Himself and of His work had been illustrated in these men.

We are allowed to infer here a fact full of help and of hope. The feeblest and most incipient apprehension of His glory by us sinners is a glory given to Him. By Him the most elementary beginnings of our under-

standing of Him and of our faith in Him are
not only not despised—they are prized; they
are beautiful, they are a wreath about His
Heb. xii. head; they are a part of 'the joy set before
2 Him,' and for which He 'endured the Cross.'
The thought needs of course its counterpoise
and caution. The comfort and wonder of it
are meant indeed to meet a weak faith, and a
love which to itself seems cold; but it must
be a faith and a love growing, or at least set
towards growth. This great utterance is no
opiate for a declining soul. It is a cordial
Psa. xc. for a soul awaking, or re-awaking, to 'the
17 beauty of the Lord our God' and Saviour.
We need at times to remember that the same
spiritual temperature, so to speak, may be
reached, in two cases, from two opposite
directions; in the one case it may be attained
in a progress upward, while in the other it is a
level explained by a decline from better things.
Rev. iii. The Laodicean 'lukewarmness' was the woful
16 condition which it was, because it was a stage
on the way from heat to frost; the same
measure of desire, of sensibility, of faith, of

love, might have been reached on a gradual
progress from frost to heat, and it would
have been unspeakably different then, for it
would have been pregnant of a better life.
For that latter condition all the comfort of
the Lord's words about the smoking flax Matt. xli.
might be appropriate; as to the former case, 20 (Isa.
the Laodicean case, we know what He xlii. 3)
thought. The insight, faith, and love of the
Eleven stood at a temperature low indeed to
what their Lord deserved of them, and to
what they were to attain hereafter. But it
was genuine, and it was growing. They had
really seen something of His secret glory,
and they were wistful for a fuller sight. So,
for all their failures, they were on the upward
road. So they were illustrations, dim but
true, of the power upon the human soul of
the vision of the Son of God. And so He
could be pleased to say, with infinite benign-
ity, yet in truth, 'I have been glorified in
them.'

Was it not so already, in the eyes of 'the Dan. iv.
watchers and the holy ones' of the spiritual 23

world?   Did not angels already bend over the little group of the disciples, as an object **Eph. iii. 10** which already had its lesson for them in 'the manifold wisdom of God'?   Surely, as angels see things, one magnificent element of the Redeemer's glory is shewn in the phenomenon of such victories of regeneration wrought in such difficult material.   He is **1 Tim. iii. 16** not only 'believed on in the world,' but believed on by hearts so singularly beclouded, and wavering, and slow.   The glory is so truly and altogether His and not theirs, that what there is of it, even when the transfiguration is only dawning in the subject of it, is pure glory, is divine.

Let us seize on this most gracious utterance then as no mere sweetness void of power. It is meant to find us out with a strong appeal to a thankful hope and, if we may use the word, to an ambitious faith.   It is meant to attract us afresh to One thus generously gracious so that we may be kindled into a new and growing love of His Name and a more adoring devotion to Him and His will.   At

'Glorified in Them'

such a call we are to return again and again
to 'look off unto Jesus,' till the soul, atten- Heb. xii. 2
tive, believing, and obeying, gets new and
growing insights into His blessed glory. So
most certainly shall our wills be attuned to
His; our 'earnest expectation and our hope' Phil. i. 20
shall be drawn out more and more towards
the peace and joy of harmony with Him.
We shall thus be delivered in happy sincerity
from the subtle falsehood of an esteem for
our own spiritual condition, by being pre-
occupied with His adorable and lovable per-
fections, which will most certainly abase us
always lower in our own eyes. And this will
be the secret way, secret yet full of the daylight of heaven, towards the state of life in
which man can reflect something of the light
of God.

It is delightful to remember that the Bible
gives us some encouraging examples of the
realization of that fair ideal, far outside the
apostolic circle. St Paul does not only look
forward to the great coming day when the
Lord will be 'glorified in His saints,' who will 2 Thess. i. 10

then be 'perfected' indeed. Writing to the Corinthians, and touching upon the quality and character of some of his missionary fellow-workers, 'men of like passions with ourselves,' in a world which was as rife as it is now of sin, and care, and peril to the soul, 2 Cor. viii. 23 he calls them, without a misgiving, '*Christ's glory.*' Then let us seek, not for our sake but for His, to reflect if but one pencil of the like light. To that end, that He may be Heb. iii. 1 glorified in us to others, let us daily so 'consider HIM' that daily and ever He may be more glorified to us within ourselves.

XI

'No Longer in the World'

'And no longer am I in the world; and these are in the world; and I am coming to Thee.'—JOHN xvii. 11.

' NO longer in the world'; in that sense of the word 'world,' *cosmos*, in which it denotes the sphere and scene of human intercourse conditioned by our mortal and 'natural' state. In the sense of the Universe, the sphere and sum of all created existence, I do not think that we find the word *cosmos* ever used in the New Testament, unless a very partial exception may be found in the words, 'a spectacle to the *cosmos*, 1 Cor. iv. both angels and men.' Practically, the word 9 appears in the Gospels and Epistles under more limited meanings; first, the visible scene of man's abode, earth and skies, the good work of the Creator, though damaged mysteriously by moral wrong; and then the human denizens of that abode, regarded almost always, where the word is used, in their character as sinners, or more strictly as a society, a system, of sin-tainted humanity, not ruled by the love of God, not subject to His Son.   These two meanings of the word seem to be both present here.   The Lord assuredly does not say that He withdraws His presence from the universe of created being.   He does say that, in some sense, He quits the scene of mortal man's abode, He quits the society and intercourse of sinful men within it.

We have here a suggestive example of the need of explaining word or phrase in the light of context.   Taken alone and, as it were, *in vacuo*, the words before us contra-vene the precious promise, 'Lo, I am with you all the days, even to the consummation of the age.'   They seem to negative, so taken, the possibility, for example, of such a pheno-menon as the voice and vision near Damascus when Saul of Tarsus was converted ; for then, as the convert himself so positively assures

Matt.
xxviii. 20

80

us, the very Lord in His risen form and frame 1 Cor. xv.
approached him and spoke to him. And 8; see the context
beside this scene, though it stands quite alone
in some respects, we may place appearances
of another type, as to Stephen in the hour Acts vii.
of death, and again to Paul at Corinth and 56; xviii. 9; xxii.
(twice) at Jerusalem; visions which had in 18; xxiii. 11
them, so far as we know, nothing corporeal,
in the sense of the scene at Damascus, but
which assuredly had in them *personal presence*. But all this apparent contradiction
vanishes before the common sense which is
so entirely harmonious with the simplest
faith, and which tells us at once that His
meaning is, if a paraphrase may be permitted, 'I am no longer now in the human
world *as hitherto*, no longer habitually and
normally here under conditions visible,
audible, tangible. To-day, to-morrow, and
for ever, I am with My people as to the
presence, yea the immanence of My Divine
Personality; and therefore, in a sense true
and precious, My Humanity is with them
too, for it is rooted for ever in that Divine

The High Priestly Prayer

Personality, which therefore bears it everywhere, though not everywhere after the manner of place. But I am no longer in the human world as heretofore. No longer am I to be sought and seen by friend and foe, on hillside and on shore, in temple-court, in domestic chamber, by the well, beneath the shadow of the rock, accessible to ever-varying converse, morning and night, precisely as mortal friend with mortal friend. No longer will My disciples be able to consult Me over every little incident of need, and to get My spoken answer—about the food for the multitude, the wine for the village festival, the money for the temple-tax, the meaning of the parable, the triumph by·faith in Me, the failure when the faith is low. Such bodily presence "in the world" is just about to cease and determine. In that respect, I come to Thee, and to Thy supreme "world." This face and form will soon, after the brief sharpness of death, after a last lingering here under conditions already half heavenly, be visible in the other and

upper world, not here. And they meantime
are and will be here, till I call them up.
And in this respect they, while they are in
this *cosmos*, will be absent from Me their
Lord. In respect of my Divine Presence 2 Cor. v.
they, by faith, will not only be with Me in i. 23
this world, but will dwell in Me, and I in
them. But otherwise, they are to be for a
season apart from Me; dwelling on an earth
and beneath a sky where they look for Me in
vain; remembering, but as a vanished past,
the day when "I was yet with them."' Luke
xxiv. 44

Such was to be the fact. So soon that He
speaks of it as if it was already over and
done, He whose daily companionship had
been the light of their lives was to 'be no
more in the world.' He was to be taken
quite away from the eyes and ears which had
grown so used to Him. What were they to
do, or say?

We can hardly with distinctness imagine
the thoughts with which, just then, at the
moment of speaking, the Lord's words would
be heard by Peter and his brethren. But we

may be fairly sure that it was with no '*joy* of faith' that they listened. That same evening, when they began to take it in that He was

John xvi. 6 really soon to go, 'sorrow had filled their heart.' And their after conduct, till the Resurrection-day itself, yes, even till its later hours in many cases, showed how totally they failed to read the divine riddle of the 'expediency' of His departure. 'I am no more in the world; these are in the world; I come to Thee;' it was a hard, a heavy saying.

Yet all the while, as we know, and as they were to know so soon, it was a saying pregnant of new, wonderful, unimagined, everlasting joy. For their beloved Lord it meant a going out of sight to a gladness and a glory which only the Father and the Son could fully understand. And for themselves it was to mean, in consequence of that 'de-

John xiii. 1 parture' of His 'out of this world to the Father,' a gift of life and power in which, while still in this world, they were nevertheless to walk as on the heavenly air. They themselves, by the grace of the Holy Ghost,

'No Longer in the World'

'not seeing Him, but believing,' were to 1 Pet. i. 8
'rejoice with joy unspeakable and full of
glory.' And they were to see thousands of
hearts awakening around them to do the
same. And they were to say to us, for
ever, in the light of their own discovery,
'Trust Him altogether; He doeth all things
well.'

XII

The Departing Lord

'These are in the world; and I am coming to Thee.'—
JOHN xvii. 11.

A LITTLE while longer let us think upon
these words, and develope somewhat
more our previous view of them; first as
regards the disciples and their experience,
then as regards the prospect for the Lord.

For the disciples, as we have already seen,
the prospect must have been sad enough,
however much they might try to find light in
it. Have you, reader, ever known what it
was to lean with an intimate and long-
accustomed reliance upon some perfect friend,
fully worthy of your trust, one who com-
bined in a noble way the qualities of strength
and tenderness, and who had allowed himself
to enter deeply into your mind, your soul,
your memories, your problems, your fears

The Departing Lord

and hopes; one linked to you by a thousand delicate ties of association as well as sympathy? And then, has he had to announce to you, it may be on a sudden, that he must leave you—perhaps for the other hemisphere of earth, perhaps for the many mansions out of sight? You have felt, if so, I am quite sure, one of the most penetrating of inward pangs; the spirit's hurt has almost wounded the physical frame as you received the intimation and began to realize the prospect. Such an experience may help us, if only by one step, to understand something of the blank, the shadow, which must have fallen upon 'the world,' for those affectionate and dependent men when Jesus was to be 'no more in it.' Did not·a cloud as of boundless night settle, in their imagination, on sky, and earth, and street, and human faces? Did it not enfold yet more thickly their inmost spiritual being, as they thought of dealing with world, self, and the evil one, away from Him—they who for three long wonderful years had gone in and out with this perfect Companion, this absolutely true and wise Leader and Lord?

> 'No more to see Thy face—to meet no more
> Till on that undiscover'd unknown shore!
> To turn to life again, and toil our day,
> Glory so distant still, and Thou away,
> While earth's dark future on us frowns, all view'd
> As one severe extended solitude!'

Such, faintly imaged, would be their outlook. And we know what, as a matter of fact, their actual experience of its apparent realization was, when for one complete day and two very long nights, between the Crucifixion and the Resurrection, they had lost sight of His presence, and as yet did not know how it was to be more than restored.

The more wonderful, the more beautiful, the more pregnant of living suggestion, is the view given us in the Acts and Epistles (if we may anticipate here for a moment) of the life of light, liberty, and divine companionship which they were yet to live. Somehow, in spite of widely differing characters and temperaments, these men, after a very few weeks, at the close of which their Lord actually did

The Departing Lord

' leave the world,' entered upon an existence in which the highest happiness which they had enjoyed at the side of the visible Jesus was indefinitely surpassed, in kind, and in volume, so to speak, and *in continuance.* What was their new-found secret, their open secret? It was—so they said with one voice, and their life amply proved it—a Risen Saviour and a living and indwelling Paraclete. And in the power of it they acted, suffered, preached, and wrote, like men to whom past, present, and future were all transformed into a ' sober certainty of waking bliss.' The past was lighted up by the triumph of their redeeming Lord, in the rays of which even their own unfaithfulness to Him was so shot through with mercy that the memory of it never, apparently, *depressed* them. The present was one wonderful experience of the quiet courage which can say, ' I will fear no evil, for Thou art with me.' Ps. xxiii. 4 And the future was changed from gloom literally into glory by the certainty of the Return of their Beloved.

The High Priestly Prayer

And this great paradox is an abiding
Gospel for our own daily need. It assures
us, for whom also, in the sense of this passage,
the Lord is 'no longer in the world,' that
nevertheless, in His promise, by His Spirit,
He is so with us 'all the days,' that *our* past,
present, and to-morrow are to be transformed
like theirs. Our life also is to shine with the
tender and living daylight of His presence, a
presence which is such, and is meant to be
such, as to be better, positively better, in our
present state, than it would be to be able
every day to visit some Jerusalem, or
Bethany, or Nazareth, and there to see His
visible features and get His spoken answers
to our words.

Such a presence as that, conditioned as we
are now, 'in the world,' would be limited to
the narrowest locality. As it is, Jesus is
with His disciple, 'at all times, and in all
1 Cor. vi. places.' The man 'is joined unto the Lord'!
17

'*And I am coming to Thee.*' So He says
again, just below, ver. 13, '*Now I am coming*

The Departing Lord

to Thee.' Let us listen, love, and worship.
Here, to our Lord Jesus Christ, was the
supreme 'joy set before Him.' In a little Heb. xii. 2
while, after the unfathomable but narrow
gulph of the Passion, He would 'go into I Pet. iii. 22
heaven, angels and authorities and powers
being made subject unto Him.' He would
be received with that sublime triumph adum-
brated in Rev. v., in which at length we hear
sounding the anthem of all creation in all its
depths and heights. He would mount to
where the redeemed nations would for ever
pour out in thanksgiving to Him the un-
ending song of their redeemed life and bliss.
But to the SON there was a joy above and
beyond even the joys which were given to
Him out of the bliss of His angels and His
saints. The heaven of all heavens to Him was
the embrace and welcome of the FATHER;
'I am coming TO THEE.'

'No one knoweth the Son but the Father.' Matt. xi. 27
In the same transcendent sense, we may even
dare to say, 'no one loveth the Son but the
Father'; no mind, no heart, save the Supreme

91

could or can know all His immeasurable love-
ableness, all that He is in Himself, all that
He has borne and has done in glorifying the
Father's love through Incarnation, Passion,
Resurrection.

Let us learn so to sympathize with Him
whom we love as to rejoice with Him in this
joy, forgetting for the moment even the
mercy of His benefits to us in the thought
of the infinite rapture reserved for Him upon
the Throne. And there need be no fear for
ourselves, as if we could be forgotten upon
that height. For He is gone up there to be
Acts vii. ours for ever—'the Son of MAN at the right
56 hand of GOD.'

XIII

The Holy Preserver

'Holy Father, preserve them, in Thy Name which Thou hast given Me, that they may be a unity ($\check{\epsilon}\nu$), even as We are.'—JOHN xvii. 11.

WE note here first a question of 'reading.' *'Thy Name which* Thou hast given Me.' The difference will be observed at once between this and the reading followed in the Authorized Version: 'Keep through Thine own Name *those whom* Thou hast given Me'; words undoubtedly more in accord with our Lord's phraseology elsewhere. But the textual evidence for the other reading, that represented in our version above, is fairly decisive.

'Holy Father.' Let us listen and worship, while the Son of God and of Man thus speaks on the eve of His 'ceasing to be in the world' and going home to the Father's

presence. Is it only fanciful to trace a special fitness and suggestion in *the adjective* here? May we not rightly think that the mind of the Son, just because He has uttered the thought that He is 'now coming' to His Father, rests with peculiar consciousness on the holiness of Him to whom He comes? The *created* spirit, human or angelic, is continually seen in Scripture to be possessed with just that thought the nearer it moves to God. The great saints of both Testaments — Abraham, Isaiah, Peter, John—are most possessed by the impression of the eternal Holiness precisely when they are consciously nearest to the eternal Person. **Isa. vi. 3** The Seraphim in the prophet's vision and the **Rev. iv. 8** Cherubim in the Apocalypse alike chant forth an adoring 'Holy, Holy, Holy,' in their wonderful and blissful nearness to the throne. And we may be reverently assured that to the Lord Jesus Himself, in like manner, according to His unique and perfect knowledge of the Father, there came with a peculiar fulness and glory, as He now prepared to depart, just such

The Holy Preserver

divine impressions as made the word 'Holy' necessary at that hour to His lips.

Let us pause for a few moments here for a recollection and resolve. In this as in everything let our Theism be governed by the Theism of our incarnate Lord. Through *His* eyes we must look upon the glory of God, if we would see it aright, and if we would live while we see. And let this particular aspect of His Theism, the aspect given us here in the word 'Holy,' be much upon our minds just now. Somewhat specially at present Christian thought is being invited to entertain views of God and of Man which claim to emphasize 'the humanity of God and the divinity of Man.' Such phrases may possibly be used without violation of the revealed faith, which does indeed wonderfully open up to us links and sympathies between the eternal Nature and the being which God created in His image. But for most minds certainly such words as I have just quoted will inevitably suggest speculations which merge the Divine and the Human into one ultimate Life. What can they practically mean but that God, if the phrase may be ventured, is man in disguise, and man is God in disguise? And room can scarcely be left in such a system for man's adoration of a transcendent and ultimate Creator, and for his abasement of himself as a sinner before the awful Holiness of a Maker's will. Whatever else we do with such 'other Gospels' let us bring them to the feet of our Lord Jesus Christ, the Christ of Holy Scripture, who is His own self-evidence, His own credential as being all true and all truthful. There let us look up from them again as only sinners, penitent and believing, can look up. We shall see there a God who is indeed infinitely sympathetic with us, who is immanent in us, as He is in all His works, but who is also transcendent over us, and transcendent supremely in this, that He is 'Holy, Holy, Holy.'

'An inadequate view of sin lies at the root of every grave religious error in the history of the Church.' These true words were never more in point than they are at this day.

The Holy Preserver

And do we wish to learn, and to retain, anything like an adequate view of the sinfulness of sin? Let us keep close to our Lord Jesus Christ, that we may see ourselves more truly as we are in the light of His awful and blissful purity—and then let us listen to Him as He 'lifts up His eyes to heaven' and says, 'Holy Father.'

Unspeakable is the difference, as regards our perceptions of the highest truths, between our condition when we take them for examination into the lecture-room—still more, into the periodical, or into the chance talk—and when we take them into our true sanctuary, the recollected presence of the Lord Jesus Christ.

But now, from this His holy Father, what does Jesus Christ ask in the words before us? '*Preserve them, in Thy Name, which Thou hast given Me.*'

'Preserve them.' The Greek verb beautifully suggests the 'preservation' which comes through faithful and attentive '*watching*.' The Lord asks for a care which means that eyes of

The High Priestly Prayer

love are upon His disciples, and that the un-
wearied action of the hands guided by those
eyes is around them. He asks for incessant
recollection, for the sort of protection called
for by possessions which are both precious
to the owner and in constant risk of injury
or loss. Nothing less is needed for these
disciples. And nothing less is asked them
by their heavenly Friend. And nothing less
was to be given to them, to the last. Day
by day, year by year, till one by one they
fell asleep, this should be the secret safety
of Peter, and John, and Thomas, and their
brethren : the watchful custody of the Father
of their Lord, never letting them get out of
sight and out of hand.

And that custody was to act in a certain
way, and within a certain sphere: 'In Thy
Name.' The Authorized rendering, 'through
Thy Name,' is full of truth, but it is not close
enough to give the truth here. The words
place before us as in a living picture the
disciples gathered and folded, as it were,
into 'the Name,' and kept under the divine

safeguard there. And what is 'the Name,' in the deep scriptural sense of the word? It is the revealed Self of 'the God and 1 Pet. i. 3 Father of our Lord Jesus Christ.' It is the Paternal Heart, known and felt through the Incarnate 'Son of the Father's love,' and giving itself to be for ever the Home and Sanctuary of human souls. That 'Name' the Father had 'given' to the Son, as the glorious Message which was to be conveyed through His Person, His work, His word. And now they were to be 'kept' within it, and to live, and grow, and rejoice, and conquer within it, as they knew, with God-given insight, what it was to be, in Christ, the own dear children of the Father of their Lord.

XIV

Unity in the Name

'Preserve them, in Thy Name which Thou hast given Me.'
—JOHN xvii. 11.

WE just now briefly commented on these
words, and explained the last clause
to mean that 'the Name' was 'given' to the
Son as message is given to messenger, or as
a secret is given to him who is to convey
it and unfold it. So it was indeed with the
'Name,' the inmost and essential Character
of Him who sent His Son to reveal Him.
However largely and wonderfully in the
earlier ages 'the Name' had been intimated
and suggested, by revelation to and through
patriarch, prophet, psalmist, by means of
things natural and supernatural, it was Jesus
Tim. i. Christ who 'brought it out into the light.'
10 That God is Love, and that God is the Father
(in a sense infinitely genuine and tender) of the

Unity in the Name

Son, and in Him of the 'many brethren,' Rom. viii. 29 was the great disclosure reserved for the Christ of God to make. And indeed He made it, by word, by work, by Person. He was, and He for ever is, the one 'express image' of Him who eternally is His Begetter. In Him, the elder Brother, we see the Father in His whole character, while we know just this one wonderful fact more about Him, that He is the FATHER of the Well-beloved.

And now 'within' that Name the disciples are to be 'preserved,' to be *watched* and shielded, as by a Keeper who will never slumber. *'In Thy Name'*; within the sanctuary of it, within the light of it, within the life and the living influence of it. The words mean a wonderful nearness and intimacy, a most loving shelter, a place and an existence close to the voice and to the countenance of everlasting Love. They mean an always growing insight into the 'secret of the Lord,' the inner meaning of 'Abba, Father.' *'In Thy Name'*; they were never to be allowed to wander out of that Name; never to seek another name, one of their own imagining or developing; never to dream of safety or of home for their souls anywhere but within the revealed personal love and life of the holy Father of our Lord Jesus Christ. Within the mystical circle of a knowledge of God as Father they were to be 'preserved,' by the skill and power of the Father Himself. And so they were preserved, every one of **Gal. iv. 6** them, when He 'sent forth the Spirit of His Son into their hearts, crying Abba, Father.'

'*In Thy Name.*' Let us often ponder this word of the Lord Jesus. And let us not be content with seeing its exegetical bearing; let us open our spirits to its power, and abide in that sanctuary ourselves. We shall find it the secret of holiness. The most **Psa.** perfect antidote to all sinning is 'near-**lxxiii. 28:** ness to God.' Sin, entertained, trifled with, **'nearness to God** even treated with indifference, soon draws **for me is** a dense veil between us and His presence. **good'** And conversely His holy presence, entertained, welcomed, sought, remembered, wor-

Unity in the Name

shipped, will be the effectual anæsthetic to temptation, the victorious negative to sin.

Then further, and this is the leading thought in our Lord's words here, we shall find, in this 'preservation in His Name,' the deepest secret of unity. '*That they may be one, even as We are.*' Those last words must be read, in the light of revelation at large, with all reverential care. Assuredly the whole teaching of the Gospel about the eternal Oneness puts it before us as a thing ineffable, unapproachable, unique, in such a sense that it soars for ever above all possible intimacy of being and of love between creature and creature. But when that is granted and remembered, we may greatly rejoice in the thought that the Saviour here (and again below, in ver. 21) does not hesitate to use it as a true *analogue* to our unity with one another 'in the Name.' So deep is that unity meant to be, so holy, so wonderful, alike in its secret and in its results, that He sets it out and glorifies it by no less an illustration than this, which

The High Priestly Prayer

is supreme. True Christian oneness is not only oneness as branch is one with branch in the tree, or as limb is one with limb in the body; it is oneness as the Father and the Son are one.

'*That they may be one*'; '*that they may be a unity*' (ἕν): so perhaps we may render the Greek. Not *a unit*; not so as for one moment to merge their personalities into one entity; let this be watchfully remembered; the remembrance will keep us from many mistakes. No, but indeed *a unity*, an organic aggregate and result, a harmony profound and beautiful, in which the parts are truly distinct yet always perfectly related. Each is *itself*, but it is itself in such a state, with such capacities and such results, for itself and for the whole, as could never accrue to it outside such a relation.

Such was, and such is, our dear Lord's intention not for His holy Apostles only, but (ver. 21) for all His own; 'that they may be one, as We are.' Unity, great and sacred word—how shall we exalt it worthily?

Unity in the Name

Alas, the controversies of Christendom check too often our freedom in speaking about it. From many sides difficulties and dangers connect themselves with the thought. Too often it is considered less in its essence than, so to speak, upon its surface, and Christians hurry prematurely to discuss the thorny problems of external unity, and some make too much of such unity, and some too little. This is not the place to enter on the question of the relation between organic unity and exterior uniformity, and on the possibility of better things than those presented by the 'unhappy divisions,' unspeakably unhappy, of our Christendom to-day. Rather, in full remembrance of such questions, and longing to contribute our little item to their solution, let us here step behind them all into 'the secret place of the Most High.' **Ps. xci. 1** What was the idea of our Lord Jesus as to the inmost and operative secret of the oneness of His followers? It was primarily and profoundly spiritual and divine. It was that they, these individual souls, should all, by divine power, be 'preserved within the Name' of His Father, His holy Father. *There* was to be the living reason at once of comprehension and cohesion, at once of gracious sympathies and of spiritual intensity of life. The more they all lived within that circle the more would they mutually understand and love, the more Eph. iv. 3 would they '*endeavour* to keep the unity of the Spirit in the bond of peace.' There they would lose self-will in the love of God; there they would train themselves for the perfect concord which is before the throne, by a life on the way thither which, lived 'within the Name,' was lived always for others' good.

XV

The Keeper: the Lost One

'Thy Name, which Thou hast given Me.'—JOHN xvii. 11, 12.

BEFORE we leave ver. 11 one more
notice must be given to these words.
Observe their implied witness to the claim
of the Lord Jesus to be the full *and final*
Revealer of the Father's Name.

It is 'given *Him*'; *He* is for ever in
charge of its glory, to unfold it and to
convey it; and He holds that charge in
such a sense that He can go on to say, in
the same breath, to Him whose Name
He thus carries to His disciples, 'We are
One.' We can never weigh too often or
too reverently the self-glorification of the
Lord Jesus, of which this is just one instance by the way. In His own view He
is, as our Light and Truth, the Last as well

Matt. xii. as the First.   'Do we look for another?'
3
No: just as persistently as Moses, or as
John the Baptist, pointed their followers
away from themselves, so persistently, so
firmly, does Jesus point us towards Himself,

Matt. xi. always and for ever.   'Come unto Me';
28;
xxviii. 20 'I am with you all the days'; 'I will that
John vii. they be with Me, where I am.'   'Never man
46
spake like this Man'—for no one else ever
commended himself as all-good, all-perfect,
all-necessary, and yet spoke not a discord
but a heavenly harmony to the inmost soul.

So, if we would be 'preserved within the
Name,' safe within the unveiled Self and
Heart of God, we must sit always at the
feet of Him to whom alone it is 'given.'

Ver. 12.   '*When I was with them I preserved them in Thy Name which Thou hast
given Me; and I guarded them; and none of
them perished (except the son of perishing, that
the Scripture may be fulfilled*).'

'*I* preserved them.'   The pronoun is emphatic.   He refers to that wonderful means
of life and grace which, in its nature, could be

The Keeper: the Lost One

transitory only—His own daily visible companionship in common life. He was to them the tangible and audible Teacher and Friend, whose face, whose acts, whose words, all tended to 'preserve them within' the certainty of the love of God in their beloved Lord. This was now to be withdrawn, but only to let other and even more wonderful methods of blessing have their way; only to leave the contact between their spirits and the eternal forces of life and holiness even more direct and unmistakable.

'*Except the son of perishing, the son of ruin, that the Scripture may be fulfilled.*' A question of interpretation is suggested here by the grammar. Are we to infer from the word '*except*' that the 'son of ruin' was at first 'given to the Son' by the Father, that he was once, in the deepest sense, one of Christ's own, and then that he ceased to be such? We may say with decision that it is not so, in view of the very frequent use of the words εἰ μή, here rendered 'except.' See, for one case out of many, Rev. xxi. 27; 'There shall in no wise enter into it anything that defileth, except ($\epsilon i \ \mu \dot{\eta}$) those that are written in the Lamb's book of life.' It is transparent there that the idiom means to say that whatever defileth shall *not* enter, while those who are written in the book shall enter. So here; 'None of those given to Me has perished; the son of perishing has perished."

In St John's Gospel in particular we are reminded here and there that Judas was on his way to his dreadful fall long before the crisis came; that his character and conduct had been grievously wrong in their depths. I cannot doubt that we are meant to view him as one who, in the mystery of sin, had never spiritually and fully loved the Lord; had followed Him from low motives; had been permitted to bear about a message which he had never himself received. If so, we have in him a phenomenon infinitely sad, but not sadder *in kind* than that presented by *any* messenger whom the All-seeing suffers to 'bear His Name,' and to bear it effectually sometimes, while yet the heart is not right with Him. It is an awe-striking reflection for the commissioned minister in his ministry. Lord, have mercy upon us.

'*The son of* ἀπωλεία, *perishing, ruin.*' That is the thought of the Greek word; loss, waste, ruin. The immediate reference certainly is not to the abolition of existence, but to its demolition into ruins. Of such an end was this unhappy one '*the son,*' in the vivid Hebrew phrase; he was akin to it, he was bound up with it.

'*That the Scripture may be fulfilled.*' Of course this does not mean that the ruin of a human personality took place just in order to fulfil a prediction and to save the credit of the oracle. But the prediction (such 'Scripture' as Psalms lxix. and cix. is undoubtedly in view) was the written, prophetic expression of the all-righteous will of God, bearing, at least as regarded the ultimate purpose of the Inspirer, upon the great betrayal. In effect the phrase here means 'that the declared judgement of the supreme Judge may be carried out.' It was

The High Priestly Prayer

His decree that the soul thus awfully sinning, against unique light, should awfully die. And then also, as we view the matter from another side, and consider the betrayal not now in its inner moral character but as a tremendous incident in the sorrows laid upon Messiah, it was, when accomplished, the fulfilment of the plan which assigned to Him the anguish of having for his deadliest and most unhappy enemy one from the inmost 'house of His friends.'

On this dark and parenthetic clause—for this reference to the Betrayer *is* a parenthesis, detachable from the context—let us make two brief comments, and pass on.

First, 'with reverence and godly fear,' aye, 'with fear and trembling,' let us note this dark line in the rainbow of even this radiant chapter, so full of life, peace, and love. With humble and worshipping certainty let us James ii. be sure, quite sure, that 'mercy rejoiceth 13 against judgement,' that the Judge of all the earth delights, with ineffable and eternal gladness, to forgive. But let us pray to be able to believe that nevertheless He means His warnings, and that there is such a thing as the ruin of man's soul, and that the Gospel is therefore a message not only of immortal consolations and blissful ideals, as indeed it is, but also of a wonderful rescue from a dread peril, generated by sin. Even in the High Priestly Prayer, behold a memento of that truth.

Then, let us with peace and gladness see here the honour put by our Lord Jesus upon the written Word. In our day, too often, even earnest Christians seem positively to desire to undervalue the divine authority of the Book, as if it was a fetter, or perhaps an outworn 'swathing-band,' cramping the higher faith. Well, it was not so with the Lord. From the hour of His Temptation to the eve of His Ascension His watchword was, not, 'it is seen,' but, 'it is written.' 'Ye do err, not knowing the Scriptures'; 'the Scripture must be fulfilled.' Matt. xxii. 19; Mark xiv. 49

XVI

Things spoken in the World

'And now I am coming to Thee, and these things I am speaking in the world that they may have the joy which is Mine fulfilled in themselves.'—JOHN xvii. 13.

THE parenthesis, for such it is, which speaks of 'the son of perishing' is over, and the Lord returns to the thought of those who are 'preserved in the Name,' and of the needs of their position as He leaves them, and of the provision for their needs. As we follow the next group of verses out, to the close of ver. 19, we shall see in detail what their trials and perils were to be. These men were to live on in a 'world' which would certainly 'hate' them (14, 16), as it discovered their alienation from its ideals; they were to linger on within the range of 'the evil one' (15) from whose wiles and violence they could not protect themselves.

Things spoken in the World

Then also we shall see the means provided for their safeguard, as they thus 'lived their Gal. ii. 20 life in the flesh,' and in the world, and as they not only existed in that position but had a mission in it (18), '*sent unto* the world' by their Lord.   For this whole prospect they were to be armed by the words now spoken in their ears by the Son (13), by the shield of the Father's keeping, placed between them and the evil one (15), by His sanctifying power within them (17), mediated to their souls by His 'Truth,' His 'Word.' Let us think first, in order, of that first specified gift for their help, the 'speaking,' by the Lord Jesus, of 'these things in the world.'

Observe the consoling significance of the last three words.   Very soon they were to lose their Lord out of the range of their senses, out of their physical sight and hearing.   But they were to be enabled nevertheless, amply and securely, to be sure of Him in His unseen life and work, sure of His mind, His character, His will, His word.   Before He went, they should first definitely hear 'these things' from the lips of Him who was to 'leave the world and go unto the Father,' but who, as they knew with an absolute certainty, could never change and be untrue. They should hear, now immediately, His utterance of this great Prayer, syllable by syllable, literally spoken into their ears. And then that Prayer was but the divine summary and concentration of all that they had ever heard Him say about the Father, and Himself, and them, and the Church that was to be; aye, of all which they had not only heard but seen in His life, His saving work, His grace, His love, Himself. They should be able for ever to be sure of Him in heaven from what they knew of Him on earth; sure that 'this same Jesus' was infinitely faithful to them still behind the veil. So should His 'joy be fulfilled in them.'

This thought, not too often noticed by students of the Scripture, is pregnant of 2 Thess. 'everlasting consolation and good hope.' It ii. 16 reminds us how deeply, and also how clearly 1 Pet. iii. and firmly, the basis of 'the hope that 15 is in us' is laid; not in a halo of legend, nor in a cloudland of aspiration, but in words spoken 'in the world'; in sayings and in doings as concrete and tangible as possible, events in place and time below. We ask for a rock to our feet, and God's mercy shews us for that purpose not the mysteries of a sphere as yet unimaginable, but actualities of the sphere we know; speech from human lips, works wrought in and through a human life, and death, and rising again. And again, we are here *intended and directed* to reason up from such things to the hopes and joys of the other sphere. The disciple, the believer, living now in a world alien to that sphere, is to be thus entitled to be quite sure about it, and quite happy in the certainty. He is meant truly to 'see Him that is invisible,' Heb. xi. and to hear Him that is inaudible, because 27 once that blessed Person was literally visible and audible 'in the world,' doing here among men His verifiable work of wonderful speech and deed.

117

The High Priestly Prayer

The reflection is capable of manifold application in the Christian life. Let us take it just now as illustrated by the use of those great means of grace 'in this world' which are eminently the voice of the Lord to us; and above all the Holy Bible and the Holy Communion. The Bible — you open the familiar, the well-worn Book. Does it strike you how emphatically it is the speech to you, '*in the world*,' of your unseen Lord? It is a piece of human literature; its contents are all conveyed through the manifold operation of human faculties of thought, writing, arrangement; it is the record, very largely, of human lives under ascertainable conditions of place and time. It is not a monologue from the clouds; it is a marvellous complex and harmony of things done and words said upon the earth. Yet all the while these things visible and audible 'in the world' are full of eternity. God is in them everywhere. And man is everywhere in them as the mysterious creature made by Him, capable of Him, fallen from Him, to be restored by Him, with eternal issues, dark or infinitely bright, awaiting him in the unseen. You read the Book 'as another book.' But the more you do so, with genuine openness of attention and reverential thought, the more you find that it is not as another book. It is exactly like other literature in that it was, from first to last, in human speech, 'spoken in the world.' It is quite unlike other literature, in its unique and solemn claim, wrought into its very texture and structure all along, to inform us about the world we cannot see. And both aspects unite to constitute its mystery, its permanence, its power.

Then again, the Holy Communion of our Lord. Out of its profound and manifold significance let us take now just *this* element. Its celebration, in an unbroken chain, goes up direct to the hands and to the voice of JESUS 'in the world.' To assure our sacred reverence for the hallowed Bread and Wine, we need no subtle tenet of transubstantiation ; we need only to remember that those sacred things, visible and tangible, are one by succession with the loaf and the cup of the Paschal Table on the night of Gethsemane. So viewed, the Rite is the very touch of the hands of Jesus, the very utterance of His voice. Nineteen centuries, ninety centuries, have no power to break that divine spell of blessing.

So the holy Supper, used by illuminated faith, puts us into immediate contact with the 'things spoken in the world' by the Lord our Life; 'things' of His death, His sacrifice, His victory, His life, His love, His care, His coming.

In a sense special and apart it will thus be for us a thing which, enacted 'in the world,' effects the 'fulfilment of His joy in ourselves.' So be it. Let Word and Sacrament alike do their intended work of blessing for us. Let them develope in us, in the response and reflection of our hearts, as we believe and love, 'the joy which is His,' the joy with which He rejoices over the souls He has redeemed, and with which He rejoices with the Father whom He glorifies in their redemption.

'He is no more in the world; we are in the world'; and it is a dangerous world to be in. But remember, we have heard Him speaking in this world. Therefore, we are sure of Him, unaltered and unalterable, in that other sphere. Therefore, His joy shall be, in faith and peace, fulfilled even in us.

XVII

'Not of the World' (i.)

'I have given them Thy word; and the world hath hated them, because they are not of the world, even as I am not of the world.'—JOHN xvii. 14.

THE Lord proceeds with His intercessory account of the position awaiting His disciples upon His departure, and of His provision for their need. Part of that provision, as we have seen, was to be the great gift and power of 'His joy fulfilled in themselves.' They were to meet their manifold problems, strong because happy. And their happiness was to be indeed strength-giving because it was to be His, while it resided in them, and because it was to be 'fulfilled,' developed, an ideal realized. It was to be His, because due to His presence in their hearts, and because its causes and its quality were to be identical with those which were the

secret of His. It was to be joy found in their
fellowship with the Father in the Son, and in
their being the agents for His glory in the
benediction of the world, on their way to the
eternal joy which would only, after all, be
the same joy, 'fulfilled' absolutely and for
ever.

Now He turns rather to the position than
to the provision. He speaks of their trials,
their conflicts, the hatreds and the perils in
their way. 'I have given them Thy word,
and the world hath hated them.'

The tenses are past. But the main reference of the last words assuredly is prophetic.
No doubt the Apostles had in measure tasted
the bitter cup of disdain and threatenings.
Many a time, we may be certain, men had
called 'the men of the household' cruel Matt. x.
names, when they so freely called their [25]
Master Beelzebub. But the Gospels do not
indicate the infliction of any great and con-
spicuous outrages, even of words, upon them
up to the very last; and we infer that here,
as so frequently in this Prayer, the Lord

is speaking as if the future, which lay germinating in the present, was the present already.

It was very soon to be so. A few short months at longest and they were 'to suffer shame for His Name,' all of them, in Jerusalem; and then a little later was to begin the record of martyrdom, and of those 'scatterings abroad' under persecution which are so easily written about, and read about, and so heartrending to experience. And the echoes of those first 'hatreds' were to sound all down the centuries, louder or fainter, through days of public and historical trouble, from Nero to Diocletian, from Chrysostom to the Waldenses, to the Mystics, to the Reformers, to the Huguenots, to the Jansenists, to the early Methodists, to the mission converts of Madagascar and of China; and through uncounted incidents also of private and unrecorded trouble in which 'the world,' that is to say, all social surroundings not ruled by the love of God, should seek to frighten off the believer from

Acts v. 41

his faith by some form of terror—from the
terror of violence to the terror of laughter,
often the worst terror of all.

What was to cause this 'hatred'? The
Lord Jesus answers the question here in two
forms, which are themselves only the different
sides of one truth. 'I have given them Thy
word'; 'they are not of the world, even as I
am not of the world.'

First, 'I have given them Thy word,' Thy
message, the revealing account, through and
in the Son, of the Father, His nature, His
will, His holiness and love. He had 'given'
them this; not merely spoken it in their
hearing, but lodged it in them, made it their
own, to possess and to convey. And being
what it was, and being so 'given,' it was
necessarily, by its nature, a transforming
thing. 'By means of the word of God' 1 Pet. i.
they had been 'begotten again, of immortal 23
seed.' They had come to be, in spirit and
in truth, 'sons of the Lord Almighty.' They 2 Cor. vi.
were a new race, conditioned by a mysterious 18
spiritual relation to the Father, in the Son,

The High Priestly Prayer

John i. 13 'not by the flesh, nor by the will of man,' but by the revealing, transfiguring, new-creating word. And in that new condition they were about to grow. They were to grow, in many an instance, by rapid stages, as when, under the power of Pentecost, the Eleven suddenly proved able to move Jerusalem, and Stephen, a little later, shone with angelic majesty upon his judges. It was all because 'the word' was 'given' them, and was made alive within them by the Spirit.

Thus, on the other hand, they appeared among men as those who were 'not of the world,' 'not *out of* (ἐκ) the world,' not derived from it, evolved from it, 'even as He was not of, out of, the world.' It was not that they were made by 'the word' socially repulsive, religiously arrogant, aggressively hostile towards the common life of their time. Nothing could be further from the fact. The records in the Acts which shew us under so many aspects both the private and public bearing of the Apostles before 'the world,' amidst normal conditions, always present them as men who respect others and are in cordial harmony with every friendly courtesy of society. And their practice only carried out their principles; 'as much as lieth in *you*, live peaceably with all men'; 'love is kind'; 'be courteous'; 'honour all men.'

Rom. xii. 18; 1 Cor. xiii. 4; 1 Pet. ii. 17; iii. 8

Yet, 'they were not of, they were not the product of, the world.' Their blameless and beautiful lives, never lived *on purpose to* put other lives to shame, were constantly, inevitably, a challenge to 'the world' to justify its principles and practice against theirs. They so lived as to disturb and annoy, in a new way, the man who could combine religion with wrath, greed, and oppression, or with mere self-pleasing in any form, or with the least violations of purity and truth. Their conduct, their characters, generated and developed by 'the word' of the Father, angered the worldling, above all the religious worldling, for they left him restless instead of comfortable in his own plan for a combination of 'the best in both worlds.' They were a witness for the eternal truth that if God is to have His right place in life it *Rev. xxi. 5* must be the first place; He must 'sit upon the throne' as the indispensable condition to 'making all things new.'

To the Lord, the Father was Life and Law. To the disciple, the Father in the Son was to be Life and Law. And that principle was, and for ever is, the antagonist of 'the world'—that is to say, of all and everything around us which is not subject to the loving will of God.

XVIII

'Not of the World' (ii.)

'They are not of the world, even as I am not of the world.'—JOHN xvii. 14.

BEFORE we quite leave ver. 14, a few words must be added upon its pregnant message.

i. *'They are not of* (out of, originated *from, ἐκ) the world.'* Place this in connexion with the Lord's utterance just below, 'I pray not that Thou shouldest take them out of (ἐκ) the world,' and an instructive suggestion arises. It is precisely because the disciples, as to the origin of their spiritual life and character, were 'not out of' the world that He will not ask that they should be 'taken out of' it. They were indeed, by the grace of the Father, not 'out of' it. Identical with 'the world' in the structure of their physical and metaphysical nature, they had yet received from God such a change in spiritual condition, such a new direction of faculty, so wonderful a connexion with the eternal Life and John iii. Love, that those amazing words, ' born 3 again,' ' born from above,' were true of them. Linked in a thousand ways with the world's life, no isolated onlookers but part and parcel of the homes and business of the world ; so much an integral part of the world (to think of them for a moment as when they had grown into a great multitude) that their removal would have left, even from the world's view-point, an immense blank and loss—yet they came, as to their deepest characteristics, from elsewhere, yes, from the world on high. But this very fact was the reason why they should not be taken away to heaven, but left here. They were effectually qualified to live in the world, and to work in it, precisely by the possession of a spiritual origin from outside of it. If they had been merely the best results of the world's own life and ways, an ' evolution ' from its matter and forces, where would have been their fulcrum, their $\pi o\hat{v}\ \sigma\tau\hat{\omega}$, for a divine influence in it and upon it? In their new birth and their new nature, in the hopes, fears, aims, and laws, which they drew from above, they had what the world could neither give nor take away; and *therefore* they were fit to be in it for its blessing.

Even so to-day, and for ever. Does a living man truly, and most humbly, 'know whom he has believed,' and does he therefore know that he is indeed 'begotten again unto a living hope'? Then let him see in that fact no reason to expect, or even in a sense to desire, a removal out of this world. Rather let him pray for growing grace to fit him so to live in the world as those should live who, precisely because they are not 'of' it, are qualified by a Power all-wise and all-kind to be a pure light and a wholesome salt in the very midst of human things.

ii. '*Even as I am not of the world.*' I will not dwell at length on the direct significance of these words. Only in passing let

2 Tim. i. 12

1 Pet. i. 3

us give thanks for a Lord and Saviour Who
is not 'of' ($\dot{\epsilon}\kappa$) the world: no product of
mundane causes, no outflow of mere developements of cosmical history, however vast in
depth and length; no creation of earth-born
enthusiasms, or of imaginations, however
John iii. powerful; but 'He that is from heaven.'
31 We give Him thanks with humblest gratitude for this His great glory. Beloved of
the Father in the eternal world, above all
time, He came from that world into time,
freely, and with all-sufficient fulness, as the
life and salvation of the children of time,
under their load of guilt, of sin, of mutability, of death. But a word or two may
be said upon the *indirect* importance of this
utterance of the Lord about Himself. It is
one instance among many of a very moving
phenomenon of His teaching—His use of
language which, in a certain sense, places
Him and His people side by side, as if
under identical conditions and on one level.
John viii.
12 For example, He says of Himself, 'I am the
Matt. v.
14 light of the world,' and of them, 'Ye are the

light of the world.'   Again, ' Thou hast loved Below 22, 23
them as Thou hast loved Me.'   Again, 'The
glory which Thou gavest Me I have given
them.'   The Apostles take up the same style
in many a reference to Christ and the Chris-
tian; 'joint-heirs with Christ'; 'as He is so Rom. viii. 17; 1 John iv. 17
are we in this world.'

Certain minds have found in such passages
a difficulty in the way of an unhesitating
faith in the full and proper Godhead of our
Lord.   Can He be the bearer of absolute
Deity when so many of His titles and styles
of glory are given also to the saints?   Or, on
the other hand, if all these prerogatives are true
of Him, must they not also be in the same respects true of them?   Are not Christians then,
after all, 'Christs in disguise,' waiting only
for a full efflorescence hereafter into manifest
equality with the First-born?   Must not the
dream after all have truth in it which would
make out that God and man are only one Life
under varying phases, one nature ultimately,
and perhaps going to converge in the end into
one indistinguishable consciousness?

The High Priestly Prayer

If such reflections should ever beset us, a few simple lines of corrective remembrance may be useful.

Observe first the overwhelming difference *on the whole* between the glory ascribed in Scripture to the Lord and that ascribed to His disciples. Stand back from the great picture, and contemplate for a while its main effect, its *ensemble*. Behold the Lord Christ Col. ii. 10;
iii. 11 Jesus, so seen. He is 'all and in all.' His people are indeed 'complete,' but only 'complete in Him.'

Then, more in detail, we find in many particular passages a provision made, as it would seem, on purpose to protect the unapproachable *difference* of the Lord. Take two illustrative cases. In Rev. iii. 21 we read the amazing promise that 'the overcomer' shall sit down with his Redeemer E.g.,
v. 12, 13;
xi. 15 on His throne. But the Apocalypse as a whole, page after page, from its earliest to its latest visions, shows us the numberless host of the redeemed worshipping, with an absolute adoration, 'for ever and ever,' the

exalted Lamb.   Again we find the great
words which assure us that the sinner who
'believes on the Name' of the Incarnate John i. 12,
Word 'receives authority to become' a 'son 14, 18
of God.'   But in the same breath that same
Word is glorified as 'the Only-begotten Son,
which is in the bosom of the Father.'   The
grandeur of the privilege of the regenerative
sonship and the supreme and solitary splendour of the eternal Sonship are thus placed in
a profound connexion, yet with a difference
equally profound.   And the whole effect of
the Biblical witness in this matter is at
once to draw the believer into a nearness
of absolute and living union with his Lord,
and to lay him at his Lord's feet, worshipping, surrendered, His creature, His votary
for ever.

XIX

'In the World' yet Safe

'I do not ask that Thou shouldest take them from the world, but that Thou shouldest preserve them from the evil one.'—JOHN xvii. 15.

THE world 'hated' the disciples, and would still do so. And they were 'not of the world,' even as their Lord was not. But for that very reason, as we have seen already, He now does *not* ask that they should be taken from it, rapt or wafted into that other world to which their true life belonged, cloistered in the calm of heaven. They were to be left awhile in the midst of this world's multifarious life, some of them for a very long while; and so through the long succession of generations it was still to be; disciples of Him who was not of the world were always to abide in it, for its help and blessing—only, 'preserved from the evil one,' abiding in the Holy One.

'In the World' yet Safe

A strong temptation of the Christian heart was met by anticipation in this prayer. Many have been the disciples, and in all ages, who have desired with a great desire, in face of the sorrows and the sins of common life, 'to wander far off, and re- **Ps. lv. 6, 7** main,' figuratively or literally, 'in the wilderness.' Many a sigh has gone up from the weary scenes of daily trial, or perhaps of danger and alarm, while persecution was in the air, as the disciple has thought of the dove and its wings, and has craved to 'fly away and be at rest.' Such thoughts have, as we all know, passed often into action. Sometimes they have issued in a domestic seclusion from 'the world,' within the fence of a devout home-life wholly isolated from 'society.' Or again, and on a greater and more historic scale, the result has shown itself in the rise and developement of the hermit life and the monastic system. No doubt some quite alien elements, not properly Christian at all, entered greatly into the causes of those

137

retirements, ideas of the necessary evil of the body, and so of the necessary call to mortify it in its most innocent comforts ; principles, which belong to schemes of thought altogether different from the anthropology of the Gospel. And again, there have been dreams of a 'score of merits' to be piled up by abnormal and ambitious austerities. But purer aims and longings also have at all times entered freely into the movement towards that literal exodus from 'the world' which has been the choice of many a pious soul. There has been the hope of a mitigation of temptations, or at least of a simplification of them; the fascinating dream of a peculiar ecstatic intercourse with God, cultivated in a sacred and unbroken solitude from the world. And then also the poor heart, perhaps already sore wounded by loss and sorrow, would many a time wish, with a longing hardly to be resisted, to debar itself from fresh and accumulating griefs by breaking definitely with all endearing ties, the ties which pro-

vide occasion for the nameless pangs of
bereavement. Who can wonder, and who
is entitled to condemn, if a flight out of
'the world' has been thus the choice of
innumerable Christians, especially in ages
of political and social misery, and of a
beclouded spiritual light? Nevertheless the
Lord's words here tell us that He did not
pray for such escapes and reliefs for His
true followers, but for something better.
They were indeed to 'abide satisfied,' and Prov.
to be 'unvisited of evil,' but it was to be xix. 23
not in the desert but in Him. There was
to be something better and nobler than even
the beautiful pictures which fancy can draw,
and which sometimes doubtless were realities
—the life of the ascetic yet loving saint in
the cloister, spending all his days, or her days,
in exalted worship and in ordered and tranquil works of mercy. The truest life of the
true saint was to be lived abnormally indeed
as to its source and its law, but under the
tests and burthens of the normal day and the
common life. And its hermitage, its cell,

Ps. xxxi. what was it to be? It was to be 'the secret
19, 20 of the Presence,' sought, found, inhabited, in
the midst of 'the strife of tongues,' and
'before the sons of men'; in the world as to
its outer circle but 'in Christ' as to its inner.

Here was to be the true victory of the true
Gospel; an achievement distinctively Christian. For it is only Christ Jesus our Lord
who can lead the soul along through the
crowds and the clamour of life, awake to the
interests and needs around it, alert for
duty and for sympathy, kept natural and
companionable, while yet all the while its
Col. iii. 3 'life is hid with Him in God.'

Such then is His prayer for His own; not
that the Father should take them out of the
world, but that He should 'preserve them
from the evil one.'

I do not hestate so to render the Greek
of the last clause; 'from the *evil one*,' the
adversary, the devil. The words ἐκ τοῦ
πονηροῦ do not, of course, fix the *gender* of
the adjective; it may mean, grammatically,
'from the evil' in the abstract. But Greek

'In the World' yet Safe

Testament usage decidedly favours the rendering given above. In only one place that I know of, Rom. xii. 9, is the adjective used *for certain* of abstract evil. And the words of 1 John v. 19 afford a pregnant parallel here; 'the whole world lieth in *the wicked one*'—where the immediate context, ver. 18, leaves it certain that we should render the Greek (ἐν τῷ πονηρῷ) so. There 'the evil one' is, as it were, the *sphere* of the world-life; it is lived '*in*' him, as he is its dreadful law and bond. Here, by contrast, the Father is seen 'preserving' the disciples so that they are '*out of*' the evil one; free from his malign contact and inclusion. They might feel his blows; they were indeed to do so; see for example 2 Cor. xii. 7, and Rev. ii. 10. But they were to be 'preserved' outside the awful circle of his spell and power.[1] They were to be spiritually detached from him, and thus enabled to be more than conquerors over him. Only, not in their own strength,

[1] I see that this is exactly the view of Bishop Westcott on 1 John v. 19.

141

even so.   They were to be 'kept within the Father's name.'   They were to be united with the very life of the Eternal Son; 'joined unto the Lord, one spirit'; '*out of*' the evil one, because safe involved '*in Him* who gave them power.'

1 Cor. vi. 17

See Phil. iv. 13

XX

Consecration in the Truth

'Of the world they are not, even as I am not of the world. Consecrate them in the truth; Thy word is truth.'—JOHN xvii. 16, 17.

UPON verse 16 I offer no detailed exposition; it is the verbal reiteration of the last part of ver. 14. But for that very reason it commands of course the double attention of the disciple. This second assertion of the spiritual *origin* of the Apostles, their regeneration from another and eternal world; this repeated connexion of that truth with the truth of their Lord's advent from that world into this, and His life in this world in the power and on the principles of that other, must indeed be meant for our special admonition and uplifting. And again, the words demand our study in regard of their connexion. Why are they thus said over again?

The High Priestly Prayer

The reason, as far as I see it, lies in the next verse. Just because of their spiritual origin, because of their being thus natives of the better world, they would need, to an intense degree, divine power on them and in them in order to make it possible that they should live out on earth the life of the child of heaven. The new nature was divinely theirs. But that did not mean that for one moment they could live the new life in it without the ever-present grace of their Father. Rather it meant the very opposite; so truly was that nature strange and exotic to the conditions of 'the world' that the bearer of it must gasp and expire here, as a spiritual being, if the Father did not surround him with the atmosphere of truth and power from above.

So we reach the prayer of ver. 17 : '*Consecrate them in the truth ; Thy word is truth.*' I have rendered the Greek verb by 'consecrate' rather than 'sanctify,' and this for a practical reason. By association, in common religious language, we connect the word 'sanctify' more immediately with the word 'consecrate'

Consecration in the Truth

with internal and subjective purification. And it seems to me that here we have in view that objective and, so to speak, external hallowing in which the God of grace claims for Himself, and sets apart for Himself and for His service, man's being and will. The issue of that hallowing, as man by grace responds continually to it, will most surely be an internal cleansing, deep and wonderful, by which the human will shall more and more gladly and fully come to be one with the will of God. But the first and leading thought here is the putting forth of the Master's claim effectually on the servant. The main evidence for this is to be seen just below, in ver. 19; of which more will be said when we reach it. There the Lord, speaking of His own sacred self, uses the same word; 'for their sakes *I consecrate* (ἁγιάζω) Myself.' In such a connexion, where the Holy One is Himself in question, no reference to internal purification is conceivable; *that* Being could not need to be made personally better. The meaning therefore must necessarily be that

The High Priestly Prayer

He was perpetually *consecrating* His sinless
life to the work of our redemption, to the will
of the Father, to the purpose that He should
suffer for us, and live for us, and live in us.
Here then, in this so near context, we
cannot err in seeing the same thought. The
Lord prays that the Father will claim them
and keep them always as 'vessels unto
honour, hallowed for His use.'

2 Tim. ii.
21

And this is to be effected '*in the truth.*'
The imagery is of a surrounding, constraining,
preserving, *environment.* 'The truth,' the
eternal certainties and realities of God, these
are to hem them in and keep them safe.
'The truth' about the sin of man, about the
holy hatred of his Maker for every phase of
sin, about the wonder of His mercy, about
its fulness, about the glory of His dear Son,
about the power of His Spirit, about the hope
of His heaven—'in' this they were to live
and breathe. This, always present to their
souls, was to maintain their 'consecration' to
the will of their Possessor, for all His ends.

And then, '*Thy word is truth.*' As much

Consecration in the Truth

as to say, 'keep them in Thy word; for Thy word is all certainty and all reality in its delivery of Thy message to man; therefore it is "*the* truth" which must surround them.' And 'Thy word'—what was it, in the Lord's thought? Not precisely, to be sure, the written Oracles as we possess them; for large parts of Scripture were not yet produced when this Prayer was uttered; two or three of the listeners that very night were to be contributors to Scripture in due time. Rather, the 'word' was the Message about God in Christ, conveyed in any and every authentic form from Him; by Lawgiver, Psalmist, Prophet, in the pages of the Old Testament; by the Baptist in the desert; by the Son of God Himself, speaking and teaching, and giving substance to all He said by all He was, and did, and bore. Only after many days would all that latter wonderful 'word' be summed up in a 'New Testament' and so presented permanently to the Church. But on the other hand, for us assuredly, us to whom now the whole

The High Priestly Prayer

multifold and harmonious Book has so long
been given, the Holy Scriptures are 'Thy
Word' as nothing else beneath the sky can
possibly be. And so for us the Lord's
petition runs that the Father may maintain
our 'consecration,' above all, 'in' the
Scriptures. He implies that our spiritual
life must be at once safeguarded, cautioned,
vivified, uplifted, 'within' the power and
spell of their revelation.

Note well that 'in' *revelation*—even for
the Apostles, who were so soon to be filled
with the Pentecostal power—the Father's
'consecration' was to be maintained. Not
even 'in Thy Spirit,' says the Lord, but 'in
Thy truth, Thy word.' *There* was the
Spirit to do His wonder-work, operating
ever within that hallowed and hallowing
circle. And if it was to be thus for them,
so it must be indeed for us.

Therefore, in order that we may abide
'consecrated,' let us dwell 'within' those
Oracles and find our secret of life always
there. Let us unweariedly converse with

Consecration in the Truth

our Bible, yes, even to the end, not for contemplation only but for consecration. One most dear to me, 'without whose life I had not been,' ceaseless student of her Bible, till old age came on and sight failed, wrote to me thus, some three and thirty years ago, about her thoughts of the vital benefit of dwelling 'in the Word':—'I desire to live a life of thanksgiving, without a sigh for what I have lost. Only, I feel constant need of watching that I may not think my soul can prosper without the precious Word of God — marked, learned, and inwardly digested—just because I can no longer see to read it.'

XXI

A Divine Ideal

'Even as Thou didst send Me into the world, I too sent them into the world; and I for their sakes am consecrating Myself, that they too may be consecrated, in the truth.'— JOHN xvii. 18, 19.

THESE two verses stand connected in a deep inward continuity. The mission and the consecration have a vital relation to one another. Alike for the Master and for the disciples there is a mission, and that mission is 'into the world.' Therefore alike for the Master and for the disciples there needs to be a consecration; without the consecration the mission cannot be carried out.

Let us take the two sentences one by one with this recollection in the mind.

'*Even as Thou didst send Me into the world I too sent them.*' 'I *sent* them'; it is another instance of what we have had already more than once, the past tense of anticipated

A Divine Ideal

action. The Lord contemplates the coming mission of His Apostles, in the fulness of grace and truth, as a thing so certain and so imminent that it is as if the command were already given and the messengers sent out. He speaks as if it were already that moment, some seventy-two wonderful hours later, when, in that same upper room where the Passover had just been eaten, He came and 'stood among them in His risen power,' and spoke 'Peace' to them, and said, 'As My Father hath sent Me, I too send you,' and breathed on them, and bade them receive the Spirit for their work. To be sure He had already for three years past been 'sending' them as His messengers; but it was a mission hitherto comparatively tentative and imperfect. In the light of the passage just quoted we are sure that His thought goes forward to their Pentecostal mission and to the equipment necessary for its work. To His inner eye they are already 'preaching every- Mark where, the Lord working with them, and xvi. 20 confirming the word with signs following.'

John xx. 19-22

The High Priestly Prayer

Yes, it was for this that He had gathered them round Him so long in his life in Galilee and Judæa. It was for this that He had them with Him just now in the solemn retirement of that Paschal evening, His very last time of intercourse with them under the old conditions. 'It was good for them to be there,' as it had once seemed so good to Peter to be with Him in the calm and glory of the Transfiguration-hill. But they were there on purpose that they might not stay there. The three chosen disciples had seen the vision and heard the words of the Almighty on the mountain-top, a year before, only to descend just afterwards to the crowd gathered around the demoniac boy. And the Eleven were now grouped around the Lord, and were at that moment listening to this great prayer of the Son to the Father, listening as if they were already with Him within the veil, only in order that within a few weeks they might be at work 'in the world,' in lives laid out on every side for other men, in the temple-

Matt. xvii. 14, etc.

courts, in the streets of the city, on the highways of traffic, before the judgement-seats of priests and governors, and at length in the uttermost ends of the earth. They were indeed 'saved,' with the sublime salvation of those who were the chosen intimates of their Saviour alike before and after His great sacrifice and victory. But they were 'saved,' above all, in order to 'serve.' They were sent into the world to tell the world about Him, and so that the world might not only hear of Him from them but might in a true sense see Him in them.

For this, as I understand it, is the point of the Lord's words, '*Even as* Thou didst send Me into the world.' His mission of them, in a sense interior and deep, was to be 'even as' the Father's mission of Him. And that supreme mission was discharged by the Lord not only by so many words of truth spoken, and by so many wonderful works done, but by the manifestation in Himself of the Father; the presentation to the world, in Himself, of the character of God. Even so the disciples were to be no mere speakers, writers, organizers, ministers of ordinance, centres of order. They were to be manifestations in the world of a new character, the character of the Lord Jesus Christ. He, inhabiting their hearts by faith, was to shine out in the life which expressed the Christ-inhabited heart. They were to be such that another day it should be possible, natural, for them to say, 'Be ye imitators of us, as we are of Christ Jesus.' In them 'Christ was to be formed,' and so made visible. They were to be not messengers only but messages—'epistles of Christ,' written in characters of heavenly truth and love.

1 Cor. iv. 16, xi. 1 ; Gal. iv. 19 Phil. iii. 17

We pause a moment to remember that this is the divine ideal not only for Apostles but for every true disciple of all time. In each genuinely Christian man and woman the world is to have, in some sort, a messenger from the Lord, but not a messenger only ; we are to be messages also, as being personalities transformed and occupied by Him. And of all the needs of the troubled world to-day

A Divine Ideal

none is more pressing than the need of a
multitude of such personalities, manifestly
altered by the Lord Jesus Christ, and so, in
some humble sense, manifestations of Him.
The worst enemy of a good cause is he who
badly represents it. The best advocate is he
who is the genuine and complete result of its
principles and power.

Therefore it is that the Lord passes on to
say, thinking of His Apostles and of us, '*For
their sake I consecrate Myself.*' Wonderful
words from the lips of the sinless Christ! But
we have seen already, in a previous chapter,
something of their meaning. He consecrates
Himself, He was that hour in the very act of
doing so, to unknown sufferings, to sacrificial
death, to the sojourn in the Unseen, for such
was His path to His victory for them and to
His 'indissoluble life' within them. He was
setting Himself apart from every other aim, and
from every sinless reluctance of His perfect
sensibilities, so to suffer and so to overcome.
And this was precisely in order that they too,
in the peace of His salvation, in the power

of His Spirit, in the fulness of His life, fired
into victorious love by His example, and by
Himself, might in their turn be self-conse-
crated ' in the truth,' in the reality of what
He would be to them for ever, for a life of
labour, witness, and the Cross, as His *messages* to the world.

XXII

'Not for these only'

'Nor for these only do I make request; but for those also who believe through their word on Me; that they all may be one.'—JOHN xvii. 20, 21.

A FEW remarks on verbal points have to be made here.

'*I make request*' (ἐρωτῶ). As in ver. 9, the verb indicates the sort of 'request' which is the 'desire' of the equal rather than the petition of the subordinate. It takes us very near to the Secret Place where the Son holds converse with the Father, not before but upon the throne.

'*Those who believe*': — not (as in the Authorized Version, based on the Received Text) 'those who *shall* believe.' The present participle is the unquestionably right reading. It leaves the sense, to all practical purposes, undisturbed; no doubt can be felt for a moment that the Lord has in view the whole

The High Priestly Prayer

host of believers in all their generations to the end. But the present tense, as distinguished from the future, not only includes the numerous converts whom the Apostles had already won to some measure of faith; it also lifts the thought, as regards all believers of all time, above the idea of days and years into that of character. Whenever such men and women lived, or should live, their *character* is always this, 'those who believe.' So the like present participle is used of 'the sower' (ὁ σπείρων) in Matt. xiii. 3, and of the great 'Rescuer' (ὁ ῥυόμενος) in 1 Thess. i. 10.

We can now take up the words before us for their message. ' *Not for these only do I make request.*' We have already, in many previous places, ventured to apply to all true believers very much of the Lord's thought and 'request' for the Apostles. The warrant for this lay waiting for us in this verse. No doubt a perfectly definite first reference to the needs and call of the Eleven runs through all we have read thus far. But also, almost all along, it has been so phrased as to bear a

secondary reference to *the disciple* in general.
And here expressly the Intercessor tells us
that He has meant it so.

For if I read this place aright He looks
backward as well as forward here, and implies that for all believers He is asking not
only that they should be one but that, for
that very purpose, in order to their becoming
a living unity, they too (like the Eleven, their
prototypes) should be 'kept in the Father's
Name,' and should be 'not taken out of the
world but preserved from the evil one,' and
should be 'sanctified in the truth.' All this
was to work inward, and then to work outward, so as to produce the splendid effect of
a mighty influence upon the world put forth
by the unification of the believing company
in all its generations. But the unity with its
influence, though of the first rank in the
Lord's purposes, was not the first direction
of His request. His request was first, immediately, directed towards a divine means
to the divine end: it asked for the keeping
and hallowing of these believing souls

in the Name and by the power of the Father.

This reflection will aid us at once to understand aright the sort of unity of which primarily He was thinking. In our next chapter we shall say more of this. But we may notice here that the whole drift of the 'request' is *primarily* towards a unity which is the effect of strictly spiritual causes, and which accordingly will show itself *primarily* in spiritual manifestations. The thought of a unity, practicable, observable, ordered, a unity which both issues from and developes a conviction of the fatal mischief of discord and collision between Christian men and between Christian communities, lies close to the heart of the deeper reference. But it is all important to put that deeper reference in its dominant place, and to keep it there. The 'oneness' is above Eph. iv. 3 all things a 'oneness of the Spirit.' It is the resultant of the sanctifying power of the Father upon His dear children. It rises from the immediate contact, in the life which Rom. viii. 15 'cries Abba, Father,' between regenerate man and God. Out of this springs the unity; the unity is not the means to this but its result.

And now, in all simplicity, gratitude, and reverential gladness, let us take those words up, and take them home; '*I make request for all who believe on Me through their word.*' We have been listening, as if just outside a curtain, to the voice of the High Priest interceding on its other side. We have thought of Him as standing within that curtain, with eyes uplifted to the unseen heaven, encircled by Peter, John, James, and their companions; and our hearts have burned within us over His requests for them. But listen now; the voice goes on, in the same tone of love and of authority, and it is speaking about us. Such is His heart that we too have room and home within it. Upon His breastplate, Exod. and upon His shoulders, there is place for xxviii. many more than eleven names; there is 12, 21 place for ours. For us He is 'requesting'; and we try to realize as we listen what the immeasurable value and operative power of such 'requesting' is. Too often our own

faintness and unbelief in intercession, our
own too easy acquiescence in at least a
seeming uselessness and failure in the work,
sadly reflects itself upon our thoughts about
the intercession of our High Priest. But
now we will cast out all such views, and
will resolve to remember that the Father
John xi. 'heareth Him always.' His requests are
42 an almighty force. And they are for us.

For us? Literally for us, in this modern
world, in this late and disheartened age,
when every sort of foundation seems to be
Heb. xii. shaken? Yes; for the one 'Thing that
27 cannot be shaken,' the Lord Jesus Christ,
gives us His word for it. Do we answer
His description, 'they that believe on Me
through their word'? Let us not torment ourselves by asking whether we meet the description absolutely, ideally; whether we are
perfect believers, untroubled by a doubt. Not
so; that can only push us back again into the
deep waters. This Intercessor is no hard
judge of our troubled souls, when they are
seeking Him. Does He see us feeling, with

'Not for these only'

Peter, 'Lord, to whom shall we go? Thou John vi. 68 hast the words of eternal life.' Does He see us finding in Him, '*through their word*'— in Him, the Christ not of our imaginations, or of our philosophies, but of '*their word*'— the Refuge, and the Life, and the Master, to whom we gravitate as the one possible answer to our needs? Then, looking quite away from our faith and quite simply upon Him, let us listen in peace to His words and take them home. To do so is the opposite of presumption; it is submission. Lord, for me Thou dost make request; to doubt it is to ignore Thy explicit utterance; for I too am one of those who believe on Thee through their word.

XXIII

Unity (i.)

'That they all may be one, even as Thou, Father, art in Me and I am in Thee; that the world may believe that Thou didst send Me.'—JOHN xvii. 21.

WE have studied the Lord's assurance that for us also and not only for the Apostles He was pleading as the great High Priest; and we have seen reason to think that for us as for them He had been all along asking those blessings of 'keeping' and of 'hallowing' of which the Prayer had said so much. Here, expressly and emphatically, for all believers, He gathers up His whole request into its highest and noblest issue. He asks that they, that we, as the result and sum of all spiritual blessing, may be one, and, yet again that we may be one in such a sense, and in such a manifestation, that the world may

Unity

believe that He is the supreme Apostle, the true and final Sent One, of the Father.

That thought fills and glorifies this whole section of the Prayer. We will anticipate future Readings in some measure to remind ourselves of this, quoting in advance from the two following verses (22, 23):—

'And I—the glory which Thou hast given Me I have given them, that they may be one even as We are one, I in them and Thou in Me, that they may be perfected into one, that the world may recognize that Thou didst send Me, and didst love them as Thou didst love Me.'

We shall need, of course, to speak of these great verses in future pages. But we must place them before us at once, that we may better feel the weight of our present verse in those weighty elements of its message, the Lord's estimate of the importance of unity among His people, and the cause of that unity, and the quality of it, and the intended effect of it in the world.

First then it is amply plain that in His

judgement the oneness of His believing disciples is an interest sacred and momentous beyond expression. Three times over within three verses comes the word : 'that they all may be one'; 'that they may be one'; 'that they may be perfected into one.' He most assuredly does not ask that they may be a *unit*; a mass of being, so to speak, in which person, in which individual, is lost. This is never His teaching; this never can be the issue of His teaching, in which the individual soul is seen to be inestimably precious, so that He, the Shepherd, leaves the many sheep for the wandering *one*, to rescue it and bring it home. Far rather His teaching, fully received and fully operative, deepens and amplifies the individual life into its noblest, fullest, and freest ideal, so that the highest possible type of personality is that of the true man truly and wholly filled with Christ. But while the thought of the *unit* is banished from the plan of His Church the thought of the *unity* is its characteristic glory. His Gospel does indeed make the

Matt. xviii. 12; Luke xv. 4

166

Unity

individual great, even to his utmost greatness. But the very essence of that greatness, according to Jesus Christ, demands that the man shall never *terminate in himself*, but shall exist—in an existence supremely large and good—for others, in the Lord. He is developed—that he may cohere. And coherence is to foster developement in its turn. He is to give himself out for others, and to them; he is to welcome them into spiritual contact with his inmost self; and *thus* he is to be fully a Christian. So the believing Community is to be totally different from a mere aggregation, for its constituents are to be fused into a common life which at once demands individuality and transcends it; it is a common life of love, love generated by the love of Him who is, eternally and within Himself, Love. And love, by its nature, 'seeks its bliss in another's good'; therefore love, by a most faithful law, results in unity indeed.

This reflection leads us direct to the view, gained from our three verses, of the *secret cause* of that unity by which the Lord sets such store. Great and sacred are the forces seen here in operation in order to the living and loving unification of the disciples. At the back of all is the intercession of our High Priest in all its prevailing efficacy. Then comes that wonderful phrase, 'the glory which Thou hast given Me I have given them'; words of which we shall come to think more closely later, but which at once assure us of a kind and range of gracious action of the most exalted kind. Lastly, and in deep connexion with that utterance, He prays that He may so dwell in them and they in Him, with a vital contact inexpressibly close and mutual, 'that they may be perfected into one.' The deep workings of that Indwelling are to be such that there shall result not only unity but a unity so strong, so great, so *adult*, if the word may be suffered, that it shall be living evidence to the greatness and dignity of its cause. It shall be the issue of an advanced work of grace in the individual heart; it

Unity

shall issue in advances of the work of grace in the community which shall indeed compel a reverent attention, even in 'the world.'

We come next to ask what is the quality of this unity; and have already almost completed the answer to the question. The oneness prayed for by the Lord is supremely a oneness congenial to such causes. It is a oneness primarily, vitally, spiritual and from within. It is not imposed upon the community from without, but generated within the inner life and derived altogether from above. It has regard to the action of the Father and the Son upon the saints; to the gift to them of 'the glory' given first to the Son; to the dwelling of Christ in the heart, and the dwelling of the heart in Christ, by faith. Its immediate outlook therefore rises above all problems of order, and even of ordinance; it touches immediately the life hid with Christ in God.

Not that it has not the most momentous bearing, at a second remove, upon problems of exterior unity; and of this we will think later. But the precisely immediate reference is to a 'bond of peace' and a 'unity of the Spirit' which belong to the heavenly order altogether, though they are designed with divine precision to work out magnificent results amidst the most concrete conditions of the life of this world.

For this, let us well remember it, nothing less than this is the Lord's 'reason why' for the grace and gift of unity. It is 'that the world may believe' that the Father sent the Son. And that can only take place, in any connexion with the unity of the saints, where that unity is such that it is the unmistakeable effect of the present Christ in His living power, and where it glorifies and makes visible its holy Cause by its own heavenly character of self-forgetting love.

XXIV

Unity (ii.)

'That they may all be one; even as Thou, Father, art in Me and I in Thee, that they also may be in Us; that the world may believe that Thou didst send Me. And the glory which Thou hast given Me I have given them; that they may be one even as We are one; I in them, and Thou in Me, that they may be perfected into one; that the world may know that Thou didst send Me, and lovedst them even as Thou lovedst Me.'—JOHN xvii. 21-23.

'*THAT they all may be one.*' We return for some further reflections to this word of the Lord's, this great *issue* towards which His whole Intercession so largely moves, and on which, as we have seen, He lays the emphasis of reiteration, three times within a few clauses.

It was apparent, so we discovered as we read, that His ideal of unity on the one hand has to do with the very essence of the truly Christian life, in which the individual believer is viewed as always related, even for his highest individual benefit, to the whole believing body. On the other hand the means which in His eyes are to converge upon this unity as their result are such, so deep, so high, so spiritual, so divine, that they alone are enough to indicate how great its nature must be, Eph. iv. 3 how essentially it is to be a 'unity of the Spirit,' knit by the Holy Spirit Himself 'in the bond of' nothing less than 'the peace' of God.

Such is it in its essence that it is comparable in some mysterious sense to the supreme and eternal Unity itself; 'even as Thou art in Me and I in Thee'; 'even as We are one.' And it is to stand connected by a close and vital bond with that Unity; for it is to take effect so that the Intercessor can say that He shall 'be in' His disciples, while the Father 'is in' Him. It is to be effected by the 'gift' to them of 'the glory' which the Father has given Him; words which we reverently interpret to mean the gift of a spiritual and real

Unity

sonship to God in Christ, a sonship based on that 'gift' from the Father to the Son which the ancient Church called 'the eternal, timeless, Generation.' And the result of it was to be, above all things, two convictions awakened in 'the world' as it looked on; one, that indeed the Father had sent the Son, that Jesus Christ was indeed His perfect Manifestation and Representative to man; the other, that 'Thou didst love them as Thou didst love Me.' Such were to be the 'notes' of this true Church in its unity that it was to be evident that the smile and radiance of divine love rested upon it, upon the true Family living by union with the true Firstborn. It was to be such, under this holy sunshine of grace and peace, so was the air of God's own intimacy and complacency to attend it and characterize it, it was so manifestly to 'keep the Father's command- John xv. ments' and 'to abide in His love,' that [10] men should feel no effort, so to speak, in the thought of its being, in His regard,

173

one with His Christ. It should be such that the wonderful words in which, another day, St Paul should speak of the Church and her Head, as being together, 'CHRIST,' should seem to rise as nearly as possible to the level of a literal fact. The happy company should so faithfully reproduce to the world the character of their Lord, and should so manifestly walk in that light of eternal love which had shone on Him, that 'the world' should, in a wonderful way, believe in Him and also, if the words may be ventured, believe in them.

1 Cor. xii. 12

Such lessons from this passage carry us so high and so far that we might seem almost to be out of reach of the very ideas of exterior order and organization. And surely no greater mistake could be made than to put such ideas here into the foreground, and to think of the Master's words as if they were a prayer, directly and as for the main object, against what we commonly mean by schism. In the field of ecclesiastical order it is quite conceivable that divisions of administration

174

and 'obedience' might be entirely eliminated, and the vast hosts of visible Christendom reduced under one all-pervading regimen, with one creed, the same everywhere in every article, one ritual of worship and sacraments, one ordered ministry everywhere the same— and yet that 'the world' might be as far as ever from believing that the Father sent the Son, and even further than ever from believing that the Church was loved by Him as His Son is loved. For the unification of system might conceivably be complete without any semblance of an all-pervading presence of the God of holiness and love animating and illuminating the parts and the whole of the community. It might be a perfect organization, and yet anything whatever but a Christ-manifesting organism.

But then there is another side. Exterior unity is assuredly not the idea and goal of this wonderful passage, taken in itself. But let us not think that the idea of the passage has nothing to do with exterior unity. One thing at least is abundantly certain. Nothing

The High Priestly Prayer

more surely tends to make 'the world' doubtful, or indifferent, about the Mission of the Son of God, and about the resting upon the Church of any distinguishing and beatifying love of God, than the sight, as it is perpetually presented to 'the world,' of 'our unhappy divisions.' And no thoughtful and prayerful Christian accordingly should think of those divisions as if they were good in themselves, being rather, as they are, a great and formidable evil. Rather he should weigh with deepening attention—and humiliation—their far-reaching effects of spiritual deterioration upon the spirits which can lightly accentuate and foster them, and the thorny barrier which they present to the faith of many a not hostile observer, who turns sadly away from the strifes of 'the Churches,' saying to himself, 'Religion is the great divider.'

Alas for the policies that aim at party victory and sectarian gain, as for *religious* objects. Alas for the pulpits whose 'Gospel,' too often, consists of little but censure, sometimes seriously unthinking, sometimes altogether unloving, sometimes recklessly untruthful, of other Christians, and their worship, and their order. May the blessing of God rest, as assuredly it will, on all His children who, from every side, adoring Him in His Son, 'follow after the things that make for peace, and the things whereby one may build up another.' As they do so, they will see with always growing clearness the supreme glory and good of spiritual unity. They will long and look always more earnestly for a generous but real and operative cohesion, loyal to Scripture, regardful of history, calculated for worship and for action; strong not in competition but in love, so that the One Spirit may manifestly, and to the world's infinite gain, be seen and felt to be working through one living body.

Rom. xiv. 19

XXV

'Father, I Will'

'Father, as to that which Thou hast given Me, I will that, where I am, they too may be with Me.'—JOHN xvii. 24.

HERE we first observe that the right reading of the Greek is clearly for the version given above; 'as to *that which* Thou hast given.' Not a plural masculine but a singular neuter is the shape of the relative pronoun; '*that which*,' not '*those whom*.' We have thus a grammatical parallel to the wording of ver. 2, on which we commented in its place. It is as if the Lord would carry up here into the prospect of glory the thought of that oneness of His people in the life of grace on which His prayer has been dwelling. He has prayed that they may be '*one thing*'; that 'one thing' he refers to now as '*that which* Thou

178

hast given Me.' And here further, as in that earlier verse, and as in that passage so full of spiritual parallel to both these, Joh. vi. 37,[1] we have in significant collocation the unity and the untouched individuality side by side. '*That which* Thou hast given':—the words set before us an ineffable connexion and coherence in the life eternal, such that not one of all the blessed company, the Father's love-gift to the Son, is fully himself without the rest, is ever contemplated in the ultimate thoughts of God apart from the rest. But then, 'I will that *they* too may be with Me':—the words assure us that personality, immortal and for ever developing, will never cease to enrich and vivify unity in the long life eternal. The radiant oneness which makes them 'the Lamb's Wife' will still leave them *themselves*; 'His name shall be on *their foreheads.*'

Rev. xxi. 9, xxii. 4

---

[1] 'All that which the Father hath given to Me shall come to Me, and the man who cometh to Me I will never, no, never, cast out.'

The High Priestly Prayer

'*I will.*' It has been often remarked that there is a peculiar directness, a majestic and unconditioned positiveness, about this word here. It is so. But the word itself, θέλω, would not of itself justify the thought, for we find it used in contexts where nothing authoritative or even weighty can find place; for example, when it is used in a question John v. 6 addressed to a helpless sufferer, 'Dost *thou will* to be made whole?' No, it is the context of the word, and the contrast of that context with other places, which gives it this majestic dignity. It stands here close to the wonderful intimation that the bliss of Heaven will have its essence in the sight of this Intercessor's glory; and surely He who so sees eternity and Himself cannot ever deliberately *will* that which is contingent only and may be denied. And it stands here in most moving contrast to a prayer which, within perhaps one short half-hour, those very lips Matt. xxvi. 39 were to utter: 'If it be possible, let this cup pass from Me; only, not as I will, but as Thou wilt.' 'Behold what manner of love,'

180

on either side of the contrast! In the
Agony He asks *for Himself*; He requests
an exemption from immeasurable pain, pain
unique as it was immeasurable, for it was
the pain of His soul offered for our sin;
and the request is altogether contingent
upon the 'possibility' that the exemption
may consist with the Father's glory and our
salvation. In the High Priestly prayer He
asks *for us*; and now there is no intimation
of reserve; no insertion of 'if it be possible,'
'if it be Thy will.' 'I *will* that they be with
Me.' The *accent* is as absolute, with the
autocracy of eternal love, as when He said
to the leper, 'I *will*; be thou clean,' and to Matt.
viii. 3;
Peter, 'If I *will* that he tarry till I come— John xxi.
22
follow Me.'

And then, let us not forget that the 'I will'
of the Intercession and the 'not as I will'
of the Agony are words in vital connexion
with each other. The Intercession rested
for its power upon the Passion. Only the
willing Lamb of the Sacrifice could 'ask
with authority' as the great 'Priest upon

His throne.' Lord Jesus Christ, forbid us
to forget it. Let us see with open eyes the
freedom of *the gift* to us of Thy glory, but
also, with the same eyes, let us always see
that the freedom for us meant to Thee *the
cost* of the Garden and the Cross.

But now, what is it which He thus 'wills,'
and which thus, in this tone of certainty and
prevalence, He requests for us? It is the
final bliss of His disciples, in the heaven of
His own unveiled presence, and for ever.
Let us begin here to think of this; we must
return to it again; one brief meditation is all
too little for that theme.

Consider first then the *sequence and order*
with which 'this prayer of supplicating
majesty' comes in. The whole chapter is,
from one point of view, an avenue up to it.
It is not suddenly pronounced. First we have
had the theme of the glory of the Father and
the Son. Then, in sentence upon sentence,
we have been led to the necessities of the
Church, for preservation, for sanctification,
for unity, and all in order to service in the

world; 'that the world may believe that Thou didst send Me.' So, and only so, are we led upwards to this great prayer for heaven. Here is no hasty rapture of emotions, no premature and unconsidered aspiration for repose and crowns, no forgetfulness that the 'prepared place' is for 'the prepared people,' and must be so, by the inmost law of things. God has been thought of before man; the way before the end; the Lord's work here before the Lord's joy there.

Let us remember this great prototype in our own thinking, praying, speaking, about heaven. Often let us 'in heart and mind thither ascend,' rising in the power of Scriptural revelation, used by faith, to the unspeakable bliss and glory which indeed await the people of God. Let the eternal light shine down, full and beautiful, brighter and brighter, even 'to the perfect day,' upon the path before us. But, if it is the true light indeed, it will not shine the path away into an unreality. It will light up its roughest and steepest places into what is at once a serious reality and an opportunity full of hope. It will make our Lord's glory, and our Lord's service, and 'the world' as our field of life and duty, more luminously important to us than ever. We shall remember how Jesus in His Intercession consecrated all the long track of the pilgrimage for His people, before, and on purpose before, He opened wide, in this closing and wonderful last word on their behalf, 'the beautiful gate of the City.'

XXVI

The Intercessor's Love

'I will that where I am they also may be with Me.'—
JOHN xvii. 24.

WE return to this verse, which indeed
offers inexhaustible matter for meditation and faith. Another, and yet another, of
these readings will need to be devoted to it,
if even on our slender scale we are to give
such matter its due.

Here then is the Lord's 'will' for 'that
which the Father hath given Him,' that
unity, that 'one thing,' that 'Bride of the
Lamb,' chosen, won, and brought into union
with Him, by the grace of 'Him that worketh Eph. i. 11
all things after the counsel of His own will.'
All through the Prayer the bright idea of
that unified company of the 'given' has been
before us, from ver. 2 onward; an idea sur-
rounded indeed by a haze of mystery, for

185

it borders upon problems concerning the divine will and the human will where our reasoning is soon and altogether lost; only of this we are sure, across and behind all the haze, that the sovereignty is the sovereignty of eternal and essential Love, and shall be seen to be so in perfect glory in the end.

It is a 'will' which indeed secures the supreme and inalienable happiness of the blessed company. Those who in any living sense whatever 'know' the Lord Christ now need no explanations to satisfy them that the prospect opened out here is the one possible prospect which can content them fully and for ever. To be with Him, to be so with Him as to see Him, so to see Him as to behold His glory, given Him by His Father—this is enough, and only this could be enough, to make tangible, credible, infinitely desirable, the hope of an endless Heaven. But we will return to this side of the verse hereafter. Another aspect of it will be enough to engage us now. That aspect is, the light which this 'will' of the

The Intercessor's Love

Lord Jesus casts *upon His love for us, His own.*

Observe then how this love is unfolded to us by this His 'will.' Is there any greater, and more satisfying evidence of an absolute affection than the known desire for perpetual companionship? Kindness has many degrees. A perfectly genuine and even devoted goodwill may be present where yet the proposal to have the object of it always, literally always, in our presence, in our company, would be repugnant, nay, would be impossible. Feelings far warmer than goodwill may animate us; a cordial friendship, a great personal liking, a strong and admiring regard; and yet the invitation to spend life, week by week, day by day, hour by hour, in constant personal intercourse with our friend would not be quite welcome; it would be oppressive; it would be too much for heart and nerve. No, it is only where affection has achieved its perfect work that such a thought finds perfect place. It is only where deep hearts meet fully, and are made one, that the prospect of a literally inseparable co-existence is sweet. But where they have so met, it is not only sweet; it is a necessity, if the two lives are to be quite at rest.

And behold, this is the thought, the plan, the prospect, of immortality for the heart of the Lord Jesus Christ. He anticipates for Himself (as He did above, ver. 5) the supreme bliss of being 'glorified by the Father's side,' with a glory which is eternally the Father's 'gift.' But even that bliss will not be all it is to be for Him if we are not there with Him, we men, we frail and finite creatures, we who once were mortals, and rebels too, without one claim upon His clemency. To constitute 'the joy set before Him' in its fulness, to satisfy His heart in its unutterable affection and fidelity, He must find *us* everlastingly close to Him, and in everlasting fellowship with Him. The Heaven of the Throne itself, let us boldly say it, will not content our incarnate God apart from the glad, respon-

Heb. xii. 2

sive, intimate presence of His redeemed.
Such is the love of Jesus that He finds
us necessary to Him there, and for ever.
We cannot understand it. But we can believe it. We can treat such love as absolute
fact, and yield ourselves up to love it back
again.

'I will that where I am they also may be
with Me.' Let us meditate a little upon
the words; they shine with 'the love of Eph. iii.
Christ which passeth knowledge.' For they ¹⁹
are a wonderful indirect expression of that
love. And the indirect expression of affection, the act or word which does not so
much state the affection as take it for
granted, as a thing certain, present, powerful, profoundly influential in the heart where
it resides, is often the most moving and
eloquent of all avowals. It was so when,
a few weeks later than this, on the shore
of the lake, beside the fire of coals, upon
the beach, that early morning, the Risen John xxi.
One asked Peter, once, and again, and ¹⁵⁻¹⁷
again, if he loved Him. The Lord did not

state the fact that He loved His disciple. But with what a depth of tenderness He let him see how much He loved him, in just that earnest enquiry, thrice repeated, after the disciple's love!

Even so here. He does not descant upon His mighty kindness for the men around Him, and for those who should believe on Him through their word, even for all who should answer to the idea of 'that which the Father had given Him.' But He does what is more, immeasurably more. He 'wills' that He should have their company for ever. He 'wills' not only that in some sublime abstract sense they should possess and enjoy eternal life; that they should be consciously and interminably glad, pure, and strong; reigning and ruling over sin and death, serving the purposes of God in the vast fields of action which will assuredly open to the blessed ones. He 'wills that, where He is, they too should be,' and should be there for ever. For though the words 'for ever' are not added, we know that

The Intercessor's Love

they are implied. The thought of them
lies embedded in the very words 'eternal
life,' as the gift of the Son, and as to be
enjoyed only 'in Him.' They are implied
in the very character of the Lord Jesus
Christ. He is a Lover with whom is 'no
variableness, nor shadow of turning.'
'Having loved His own, He loveth to the
end,' to the endless end, to all eternity.

1 John v. 11

James i. 17

John xiii. 1

XXVII

'Ever with the Lord'

'I will that where I am they too may be with Me, that they may behold My glory, which Thou hast given Me ; for Thou didst love Me before the foundation of the world.' —JOHN xvii. 24.

ONCE more we approach this great request of our Intercessor, this wonderful article in that 'last will and testament, to be Executor whereof He rose again.'

In the previous chapter we considered its pregnant witness to His love for us, in its depth and fidelity. Let us now see in it in turn its witness to His own personal glory. Look upon it as a leading instance, perhaps the crowning instance of all, of that continual testimony to Himself, that 'good confession' of His own Name, which is so characteristic of the Lord Jesus. Imagine the moral shock which it would be, and ought to be, to hear just these words from the lips of a creature,

1 Tim vi. 13

that is to say of one who, however exalted,
even to the utmost apex of angelic glory, yet
owed existence to the mere will of God, and
would never have existed at all but for that
will. But who feels a moral shock here?
The very words which would be high treason
from the voice of a seraph are deep, sweet
music, a perfect harmony of truth and beauty,
from the voice of Jesus. Why is it so?
It is because, in innumerable ways, to our
reason, to our wonder and worship, to our
faith, to our love, He has been 'declared to Rom. i. 4
be the SON of God,' not His creature but
His Son, Bearer of the fulness of the supreme
Nature. So, and only so, we can listen and
give thanks, as He here speaks about the
eternal bliss, and tells us what its experience
will be ; that it will be one long 'beholding of
His glory.'

We have here then one of those indirect,
inferential, confessions by Himself of His own
majesty which are so singularly impressive to
faith. It is a parallel to the prayer of the Eph. iii.
Apostle, that we 'may know the love of [19]

The High Priestly Prayer

Christ which passeth knowledge'; words which would be an invasion of the claims of the infinite God if Christ were less than infinite also Himself. Yes, this kind Friend of His disciples, this patient Teacher, this *omnipatient* Sufferer, who was just about to walk into the Garden of the Agony, and thence to the awful Cross, is meanwhile such that without an effort, without the least disturbance of the quietude and *sanity* of His accent, speaking as the affectionate Advocate of His followers on earth, He asks that they may be permitted to see Him in His glory, because that sight is Heaven.

He can ask *nothing greater* for them than this, as He moves here to the climax of His final and supreme request. Then truly 'Thou art the King of Glory, O Christ; Thou art the everlasting Son of the Father.'

Even so—the everlasting SON. Here is that other radiant side of the mighty mystery of the faith. He who thus speaks cannot be less than God, cannot but be infinite, absolute, eternal. But also, so He equally and always reminds us, He is God the Son. He is no creature, contingent upon a will which might have willed Him *not* to exist; He is 'necessary'; that is to say, Deity would not be Itself without Him. But in Deity, always, eternally, above all time, 'before the foundation of the world,' in an order of *being* that transcends all *becoming*, He is the Son. Eternal as the Father, He is eternally *of* the Father, as stream is perpetually born of fountain, as day of sun. Eternally the paternal Love, unbeginning and unfathomable, is upon Him and about Him. Eternally the filial Love, in its glorious response of co-equal greatness, goes forth to the Father, and delights to glorify the Father to those who, in the Son, are children of their God.

How shall we speak of it? How shall we be silent about it? Have we caught, through heavenly grace, the least glimpse of *the beauty* of our Divine Redeemer? Have we in any real measure apprehended the divine warmth of the thought that He is 'the BELOVED

The High Priestly Prayer

Matt. iii.
17; xvii.
5
SON'? If so, we have begun, however feebly, to understand Him in this prayer for us. We have begun to see how deep the light lies within the words in which He indicates our coming Heaven — a Heaven in which the sight of Him as God, and of Him as Son, of Him in the Father and of the Father in Him, Ps.
xxxvi. 9 will be our 'Fountain of life,' will be that 'Light in which we shall see light' in everything that eternity can shew us.

As we close, turning from this wonderful verse only to return to it ever and again in our thoughts and thanksgivings, let us 1 Cor. xv.
49 humbly rejoice that 'the Heavenly One' gives us here, as His own account of heaven, just such a view, couched in just such terms. He leads us up in mind to an existence which, when we come to details and try to shape them in imagination, is altogether 1 John iii.
2 beyond our touch of thought. 'It doth not yet appear what we shall be,' nor how we shall be, nor, when we try to think out *localities*, where we shall be. Probably, our best and apparently soundest speculations on

these problems may be found, in the first moment of experience beyond death, wide of the actual mark—not only short of it, but wide of it, by immense degrees.   But what the Lord does here is to let us understand quite clearly that our bliss will be perfectly secured by being with Him, and by beholding Him. Within those thoughts, and around them, lie possibilities of infinite richness and variety. But in themselves they are simplicity itself. And it is a simplicity exactly adjusted to the needs of the heart which has begun here below to find in Jesus Christ, Human, Divine, Personal, Present, 'all its salvation and all its desire.'   Then let us bless Him for this wonderful Request and the vast yet tender Promise which it enfolds.   And let us address ourselves to the next step up the hill of the pilgrimage, at whose summit is the Presence and the Vision.

2 Sam. xxiii. 5

God be thanked for the reiterated assurance of a heaven so happy, so inexhaustible, so credible.   'To-day thou shalt be with Me'; 'Lord Jesus, receive my spirit'; 'We

Luke xxiii. 48; Acts vii. 59; 2 Cor. v. 7, 8; Phil. i. 23

shall ever, always, (πάντοτε) be with the Lord'; 'To depart is to be with Christ,' 'to get home to the Lord,' 'walking,' at last, 'by sight.'

Well has it been written by that true seer and singer, Frances Havergal :—

> 'Our fairest dream can never
>   Outshine that holy light ;
> Our noblest thought can never soar
>   Beyond that word of might ;
> Our whole anticipation,
>   Our Master's blest reward,
> Our crown of bliss, is summ'd in this—
>   *" For ever with the Lord."* '

XXVIII

The Righteous Father

'O righteous Father—and the world did not know
Thee; but I knew Thee, and these men knew that Thou
didst send Me. And I made known to them Thy name,
and will make it known; that the love wherewith Thou
lovedst Me may be in them, and I in them.'—JOHN
xvii. 25, 26.

A FEW words may be said as to the tenses
used in the translation above. I have
written, 'did not know,' rather than 'hath
not known'; and so throughout the passage.
There are many places in the New Testament in which it is obviously right to use
the English perfect for the aorist of the
Greek, a rightness which lies in a difference
in the genius of the languages. But this is
not such a place, for the retention of the
aoristic '*did know*' is here perfectly con-
sonant with the point of view of the whole
Prayer. As we have seen in previous pages,

the Lord speaks in this great sacerdotal
Intercession all along as if the sacrifice were
over and done, the work of death finished,
and the Holiest Place already entered. In
just that sense He here, by a sublime
anticipation, *looks back* upon 'the days of
His flesh,' and sees their experiences gathered
up and isolated from the present. Even so
His Apostle another day was to *anticipate
the retrospect* of his glorified spirit, and to
say, 'Then shall I know even as *I was
known.*'

1 Cor.
xiii. 12

It is profoundly impressive, this supreme
and calm review of His incarnate experience,
made *just before* the Agony, the Cross, and
the Tomb ; this implied absolute consciousness of a predestined completeness and
success. And it is most impressive when
we best remember what was almost at once
to follow in fact, beneath the olives, across
the Cedron. Astonishing contrast, yet
deepest harmony ; this serenity and this
conflict ; this divine victory, sure to be
achieved, and counted upon here as already

The Righteous Father

won; that human suffering, unfathomable, inscrutable, through which, equally for certain, the triumph was to be realized. They are two sides of the one everlasting fact of 'the salvation which is in Christ Jesus.' 2 Tim. ii. 10

One further detail of translation comes to be noted: 'O righteous Father—*and* the world did not know Thee.' The '*and*' is omitted in our Authorized Version, as it was, long before, in the Vulgate Latin. But its place in the Greek is quite certain. What is the point of it? If I see it aright, it practically means what '*yet*' would mean; it marks a pause and, as it were, a shock of thought:—'I knew Thee for righteous—*and*, for all that, the world is blind to Thy moral glory.' Exactly so St Chrysostom interprets it; and he, the great *Greek* expositor, is a weighty witness in such a case. 'The Lord seems,' so runs his homiletic comment here, 'to say this as one who was displeased that they refused to recognize Him who is so good and so righteous.'

The High Priestly Prayer

If so, a momentous import is given to those brief and mighty words, ' O righteous Father.' In a certain sense, they seem to gather up some of the glorious contents of the Prayer into one thought of filial contemplation. All through it, now in one form, now in another, the glory of the Father has been present to the mind of the Son ; and most of all in the words last uttered before this sentence. There He had spoken of the glorification of His true disciples, and how this was to find its eternal secret in their unveiled vision of His own glorification ; and that glorification, how does He present it ? As above all things, essentially, eternally, the gift of the Father, the effluence on the Son of the Father's immeasurable and transcendent love. He, the Father, is the ultimate thought in the whole blissful prospect ; ultimate, not because He is more divine than the Son, but because He is the Father, because eternally the Son is Stream and He is Spring. And now, full of that view, the Interceding Son

The Righteous Father

rises, as it were, out of His intercession into the most direct possible contemplation, and stands rapt in a conscious sight of the Father as He is. And lo, that consciousness is focussed now upon just one supreme idea, the RIGHTEOUSNESS of the Father, His Righteousness now, surely, as seen in its eternal *beauty*, the Righteousness of the *divine love*. Resting and rejoicing in the Father's smile upon His own sinless Person, Jesus Christ is inexpressibly aware that in Him who so delights in His Son law and love meet and are one for ever, and that the world, if it would but open its eyes and see, would find its absolute rest in HIM, whatever clouds should for a time surround His actions.

We may presume to illustrate the words by supposing some earthly son thinking of the character of his father when that father is slandered and dishonoured. He has had a thousand evidences in his own life of his parent's perfect union of inflexible principle with tenderest sympathies and self-sacrificing kindness. Some firm refusal to do wrong, some refusal perhaps to hurry where delay was duty, to speak where silence was wise, has exposed him to loud reproach. And his son, who is also his inmost friend, exclaims, in face of the misunderstanding, with a great intensity of loyal devotion, 'My father is absolutely in the right and wholly kind; where he is silent, I must be silent too; I am not free to tell you about his reasons as yet. But I know him perfectly, and I claim for him your entire reliance, your assurance, antecedent to explanations, that he is certain to prove kindly just and justly kind.'

'*Righteous*':—such is the last epithet given to the Father by the Son. Listen to it with awe, and with a deep peace also. Let us who by grace 'believe on the name of the Son of God,' as the Word and the Spirit have shewn Him to our souls, adore this witness borne by the all-knowing insight of our Lord. Let it be present with us when some 'great deep' of the Father's 'judgments' and His 'ways' seems ready to

John v. 14

Ps. xxxvi. 6

204

The Righteous Father

overwhelm our minds. Let it be present when grief, heavy grief, oppresses us, when we have to suffer what we call 'a *cruel* blow.' Such things have sometimes even shaken faith down into almost atheism when they have been met by the soul *alone*; the woe comes—and the Lord will not explain Himself; He will not speak. Nay, but He '*hath spoken—in His Son.*' 'Clouds and darkness are round about Him'; and He does not, as yet, bid them melt away into light. But from within them He has 'sent forth — *His Son.*' From the cloud JESUS has issued, to live, to suffer, to atone, to overcome, to love, so greatly to love. For us sinners He has gone back again within the cloud, for a season. And before so going back, He has looked towards that cloud with eyes that see beyond it, and has said, in our hearing, for our hearts, 'O righteous Father.'

Heb. i. 2

Ps. xcvii. 2

Gal. iv. 4

XXIX

Warning and Consolation

'O righteous Father—and the world did not know Thee, but I knew Thee, and these men knew that Thou didst send Me.'—JOHN xvii. 25.

'*THE world did not know Thee*.' The Lord refers here to 'the world' as He had met it and dealt with it 'in the days of His flesh,' now about to close. This reference appears certain in the light of the rest of the Prayer, in which He so repeatedly alludes to the past of His earthly ministry. It is searching indeed to observe that, if so, He has particularly in view what we may call the '*Church-world*,' the 'world' of human hearts and human life as seen not under conditions of pagan ignorance but as instructed by Moses and the Prophets, and endowed with the institutions of a true worship. Everything was in favour of that 'world,' in

Warning and Consolation

respect of the knowledge of God, so far as He had revealed Himself as yet to man. It was a 'world' familiar with the law of Sinai, with the divinely-given types and teachings of the Temple ritual, with the spiritual revelations and appeals of the Psalms and of the Prophets. It was a 'world' provided everywhere with houses of prayer and with expositors of truth. Yet of that 'world' the Lord Jesus here says that it 'did not know' the Father. So was its spiritual sight obscured and perverted by sin, by love of this life and its treasures, by self-will, by pride, by lust, that it was 'blind in the light of noon.' It recognized the Supreme Being, the Eternal; many of its members were even fanatically devoted to their creed of the One Lord. But they did not know 'the Father.' The infinitely tender and awful righteousness and love of that word had found no place in their hearts. When the Father's own Son appeared among them, to give a new and most wonderful insight into the glory of that word, they 'saw no beauty' in the Son ; how then Isa. liii. 2

could they 'know' the Father, of whom He
is the 'express Image'? He was to them
Matt. xv. 9 only a name; 'their heart was far from
Him.'

It is a thought to penetrate and to warn.
It reminds us that it is all too possible to have
around us a wealth of revealed truth, and
ordered worship, and spiritual privilege, and
yet to be quite ignorant of God. Christian
ordinances and association are just as little
able to convey saving 'knowledge' *automatically* as the Hebrew institutions were able.
They are indeed God's gifts; they are God's
acts and ways of giving; but for us now, as
for that other 'world' of old, the giving
must be met by a taking on our side, a
taking which, while it is the effect of grace, is
yet our work, the response of our spirit to the
Holy Spirit. Without that 'taking,' prayers,
Ministry, Scripture, Sacraments, incorporation into the visible divine Society, must
leave us still 'the world'; we shall not
'know' the Father, nor the Son; we shall not
have the life eternal. 'Let all be baptized,'

Warning and Consolation

writes St Augustine, 'let all enter within the On 1 John v. church walls; the children of God are distinguished from the children of the evil one by love alone; they who love not are not born of God.'

With all reverence and inmost thanksgiving let us bless Him for our Baptism, our Communion, our membership and fellowship in the visible Church, for the benefits of the ordered Ministry, for the holy written Word. But let us not think that the channel is the stream, nor dare to make the fatal error of taking privilege for life. Without the response of the awakened spirit, without the 'taking' which appropriates and realizes the 'giving,' without the 'knowledge' which is but the open eyes of adoring love, privilege is not life but death.

'*But I knew Thee.*' It is not necessary to dwell here on those sacred words; we have already practically considered them when we thought of the import of the utterance, 'O righteous Father.' But let us just once more thankfully recall the all-precious war-

rant which we have in them for a faith in
the eternal Father as absolute, as simple, as
warm, as faith can be. Behold the Son of
God, as He looks upon the Being of the
Father. Listen to Him as He speaks to the
heart of the Father. We know JESUS; He
Rev. iii. has indeed approved Himself to us as 'the
14 faithful and true Witness' in every word He
has been pleased to speak in our ears. In
Him we have found the absolute satisfaction
of that ideal of truth and good which, while
in us, *we know* to be not of us, but from
1 Cor. ii. above. He has indeed 'searched the depths'
10 of God. Into the fathomless glory, 'dark
with excess of bright,' He has passed; nay,
from it, from the very sanctuary of it, He
has come; it is His home. He, and only
He, absolutely and in all things knows the
Father. And now, in our hearing, He speaks
about that knowledge with an unclouded
brow, with a voice full of the sacred quiet of
an eternal satisfaction. And we, as we listen,
and as the Spirit makes the voice of the Son
articulate to our spirits, will enter into that

quiet, and repose ourselves upon the fact
that the Son 'knoweth the Father,' and Matt. xi.
knoweth Him to be such that the knowledge 27
is His own perfect joy.

'*And these did know that Thou didst send
Me.*' Yes, they knew this.   Imperfect indeed as yet was their knowledge of the full
glory of the Christ.   It was soon to be much
greater, in the light of Calvary, and the empty
Grave, and Pentecost; but it would be imperfect even then, for Christ 'passeth knowledge,' Eph. iii.
and will pass it for ever.   But they did really 19
know that their Lord was the supreme Sent
One, the Apostle and Representative of the
Father; not only a sublime example of goodness and greatness, the all-wonderful Ideal of
Manhood, but, along with all this, also and
above all, the Sent Son of God.   Seeing Him
so, they were on the way to all light, and all
peace, and all the joy of a divine life in Him.
They were on the way to a perfect and con-
quering faith in the Son, and to the radiant
happiness of an assurance of the Father's
love, who 'loved them, because they had John xvi.
27

loved the Son, and *had believed that He came forth from God.'*

We too, by His grace, know Him and believe in Him as the Sent One. It is for us then, even us, to enter into the deep joy of apostolic faith.

XXX

Indwelling

'And I made known to them Thy name, and will make it known, that the love wherewith Thou lovedst Me may be in them, and I in them.'—JOHN xvii. 26.

SO the High Priest closes His Intercession. And He closes it not with prayer but with a gaze fixed upon the eternal issues of His work of revelation. He is just about to pass from the exercise of Intercession to His Passion, to His Sacrifice, His Propitiation for our sins. But He first directs this expectant gaze towards what His followers, through and in Him, are to find of divine love and of a divine communion unspeakably intimate.

'*I made known to them Thy name*'; ἐγνώρισα. It is almost the same phrase as that of ver. 6, 'I manifested Thy Name'; only with the difference that the verb here

denotes a more detailed and explicit account
of 'the Name.' It implies *an explanation*
which was to make the significance of 'the
Name' not only glorious but, so to speak,
articulate. So indeed it had been. In
numberless utterances to them, above all in
the presentation to them of Himself as the
Son of the Father, the true Likeness of the
Father, He had put before them the treasures
of 'the Name'; He had turned those treasures,
so far as His own sacred efforts were con-
cerned, into 'current coin' for these minds
and souls. Point by point He had let them
know the character of His Father, till the
Lord Jehovah of the Law and the Prophets,
seen of old to be living, omnipotent, holy,
gracious, yet seen all the while through a
glowing haze by comparison with this new
sight, was brought into their view as essential
and personal Love, related to them in a union
as close as His incarnate Son could make it.

'*And will make it known.*' His revealing
work then was not done ; it was but begun.
That same sacred *explanation* was to go on in

Indwelling

the future; they were yet to know such things about 'the Name' as were to make even their present knowledge dim and elementary by comparison. Can we doubt that the Lord refers here, primarily and mainly, to what His death and resurrection were to 'make known' to them in act, and to what they were to learn from His words during the Forty Days, and then above all to what the Spirit was to show them in the Pentecostal times? For all this did actually constitute an after-teaching as to 'the Name' which was incalculably momentous. We may measure it in some degree by comparing the Apostles' knowledge, as it was shown even in the Paschal colloquies, when their questions and comments always betrayed the imperfection of it, with what it became as we can trace it in their words preserved in the Acts and above all in the Epistles. So did the Lord Jesus go on to 'make the Name known' to them that they speak of it, and write of it, as only they could do who had indeed become the very friends of God, the worshipping intimates of the Father in the Son.

May we not carry the reference of the words still further on, and reverently claim that they are fulfilling even now? Is not 'this same Jesus,' by that same Spirit, evermore 'making known' that same 'Name'? Not by adding new matter to the revelation of it, but by leading the soul, and the Church, always further into a believing insight into the glory and wonder of the already disclosed matter. Year follows year, and the Christian's view of the glory of his reconciled and most loving Father grows, under a light not his own, 'with the process of the suns.' The individual, as he 'fulfils his course' and gathers up his experience—how often he finds that it is precisely the loving glory of the Father which he sees more and more in the face of the Son! And then, in the collective experience of the Church, age follows age, and the Church, as we approach the consummation, has it not felt a parallel developement? Does not the

Indwelling

collective insight of believing man, where faith is spiritually true to Scripture, come to see not less of the treasures of the Person and Work of the Son, nor less of the tender and mighty mercies of the Spirit, but more of 'the Name' of the Father, as the Source of all, as the Goal and Repose in which all is gathered up?

'That the love wherewith thou lovedst Me may be in them.' Here is the precise and inmost aim of all the 'making known.' Supremely true to Himself, now as ever, the Lord makes all *knowledge* wholly subservient to divine *love;* and He connects Himself inseparably with all the experiences of that love in redeemed man. He cannot for a moment rest short of that goal for the souls of His disciples. It would be absolutely futile, in the estimate of Christ, that they should be only Theists, however philosophically sound, that they should be only Trinitarians, however deeply and watchfully orthodox upon the great mystery of the Triune glory. All would be vain, for all

would fall fatally short of the divine purpose of revelation, if the contact of love were not set up between the human soul and 'the only true God.'

To Him (and let it therefore be also to us) there can be no *Theology* worthy of the name that does not issue in this, for the living man who really apprehends it. That great word, *Theology*, has been 'soiled' with all manner of 'ignoble use,' till it has come to cover types and fields of knowledge or enquiry which have no more to do with a knowledge of the Eternal Personal Being than arithmetic or geography may have. But in its true meaning, in the sense of 'the Science of GOD,' Theology soars to His very heart, and there, and there only, finds its rest and life. And then, what a rest, and what a life! The man who learns that science in the school of the Spirit finds not only that he ought to love God, but that God inexpressibly loves Him. And this He finds not anywise, but in 'the Col. i. 13 Son of the Father's love.' United by faith to his Saviour, and seeing his Saviour as the

218

Indwelling

Beloved Son, he 'knows and believes the love 1 John iv. 16 of God,' and finds it to be nothing short of the paternal tenderness of the Blessed Father, who, loving the Son immeasurably, loves unspeakably the man whom He beholds 'joined 1 Cor. vi. 17 to his Lord, one spirit.' That Father's deepest love is on him, nay, it is 'in' him; it lives and moves within the soul, formative, creative, an inward light and fire.

'*And I in them.*' Thus finally and supremely does the Lord, in the act of unveiling the Father's love, embody it as it were altogether in Himself. He is eternally the Receiver, the Object, of that infinite affection. And He, so loved, is, by His Spirit, nothing Eph. iii. 17 less than the Inhabitant of the surrendered and believing heart. So deeply does He love the man that He can be content with no exterior contact, however close; He must have His personal abode in the sanctuary of the human personality itself. Into that sanctuary He carries with Him the love that was His own possession 'before the foundation of the world.' And there, from Him the

The High Priestly Prayer

Indweller, from Him in His precious imman-
Rom. **v.** 5 ence, it is 'shed abroad,' it is 'poured out,' to
fill and beautify the being.

So the great High Priest concludes the
Intercession. It began with Himself, and
with Himself it ends; He is its Alpha, and its
deep Omega too. If He were less than the
co-equal Son it would be tremendous. As it
is, it is the music of the heaven of heavens.
It speaks ultimate and self-attesting truth to
the inmost human heart, as it reveals to it
the love of the Father for the Son, the love
of the Son for the disciple, the wonderful
union of the disciple with the Son, and his
possession thus, in Him, of the very love with
which the Son is loved eternally.

As He then interceded, so now He inter-
cedes, 'ever living.' To Him be glory.
Amen.

Note

THE stanza quoted at the close of chap. v. (p. 43) is
part of a little poem written by one revered friend of
my early days, the Rev. C. W. Bingham, Rector of
Bingham's Melcombe, Dorset, after the death of
another, the Rev. T. W. Birch, his neighbour, sixty
years Rector of Cheselborne. It is quite inaccessible
now, as far as I know, and its truth and beauty may
justify my quoting it here complete. The lines were
written to put into verse-form Mr Birch's thoughts
expressed in a last interview with his friend.

> ' Life's journey almost past,
>   Tottering I stand at last
>   Close to the door ;
>   Weary the way hath been
>   And often sad through sin ;
>   Now all is o'er.

> ' The friends I walk'd beside
>   At noon and morning tide
>   Went long ago,
>   And evening's travel, grown
>   Ever more chill and lone,
>   Seem'd to pass slow.

The High Priestly Prayer

'Yet was it night, not day,
Thus slowly waned away,—
　　Now dawn is nigh :
The daystar's warning bright
Tells me the shades of night
　　All soon will fly.

'Beyond that welcome door
I know—and oh, for more,
　　Why should I care?
I shall my Saviour see
As now He seeth me ;
　　JESUS is there ! '